IGNITE
YOUR FAITH

GET BACK IN THE FIGHT

TIM CLINTON

AND MAX DAVIS

DESTINY IMAGE® PUBLISHERS, INC.
P.O. Box 310, Shippensburg, PA 17257-0310
"Promoting Inspired Lives."

This book and all other Destiny Image, Revival Press, MercyPlace, Fresh Bread, Destiny Image Fiction, and Treasure House books are available at Christian bookstores and distributors worldwide.

For more information on foreign distributors, call 717-532-3040.
Reach us on the Internet: www.destinyimage.com.

ISBN 13 TP: 978-0-7684-0493-7
ISBN 13 Ebook: 978-0-7684-0494-4

For Worldwide Distribution, Printed in the U.S.A.
1 2 3 4 5 6 7 8 / 18 17 16 15 14

DEDICATION

Dedicated to every man who is in the fight, has been in the fight, or deeply desires to get back into the fight.

To all of those men who dress for battle everyday —who stand with me—who give me strength and deep encouragement. You are my band of brothers—men of valor—true warriors with a committed cause. You know who you are...

In honor of my son, Zach, whose name means 'Remembered by God'. You inspire me every day to be a better dad and to not miss a beat in living out my faith. I am so proud of the man you are and are becoming...

LET'S ROLL.

Introduction

BACK IN THE FIGHT!

*To become a champion, fight one more
round.* —JAMES CORBETT

*Blessed be the Lord, my Rock, who trains my hands
for war, and my fingers for battle* (Psalm 144:1).

When Roberto Duran stepped into the ring for a rematch against Sugar Ray Leonard on November 25, 1980, he was the World Welterweight Champion. Known as one of the most dedicated, intense warriors in the ring, Duran had defeated Leonard by a razor-thin margin to capture the world title just six months earlier. The rematch was heavily promoted and had the boxing world spinning with anticipation.

Knowing the fight was going to be as much mental as physical, in the pre-fight interviews Sugar Ray consistently poked at Duran's manhood and self-image in an attempt to shake him up. He knew if he could get under Duran's skin, he'd have an advantage.

The fight lived up to all the hype with both boxers coming out aggressively, with great confidence. Popular and funny, Sugar Ray was overwhelmingly the crowd's favorite.

With arguably the fastest hands in boxing, his smooth style and psychological tactics continued in the ring with a lot of dancing, taunting, and laughing at his opponent in a continued effort to unravel him. Even though Sugar Ray had been able to land consistent jabs and uppercuts, at the end of the 7th round he was only leading by a small margin of 68-66, 68-66, and 67-66 on the judge's scorecards. Duran was behind but was certainly not out. Then, in the 8th round, Duran stunned the boxing world. After taking a right uppercut from Sugar Ray, he turned to the referee and said, "No más," (meaning "no more" in Spanish). Duran went to his corner and ended the fight. It was the first time in nearly twenty years that a reigning champion had voluntarily surrendered his title. Apparently, Sugar Ray's strategy had paid off. Duran's trainer, Ray Arcel was so upset he yelled, "That's it! I've had it. This is terrible. I've handled thousands of fighters and never had anyone quit on me!" Freddie Brown, Duran's co-trainer said, "I was shocked!"

There have been a variety of speculations why Duran quit that day ranging from stomach cramps to embarrassment. In one interview after the fight he said simply, "I don't want to fight anymore. I've been fighting for a long time." Sugar Ray's response was, "To make a man quit, to make a Roberto Duran quit, was better than knocking him out." Sugar Ray's relentless stream of jabs, jeers, and intimidation wore Duran down physically and mentally.

Just like a champion boxer, if you're a Christ follower, you're engaged in the fight of your life against a very real opponent, one who would love to knock you out. Yet this enemy knows that with God's Sprit inside of you he can't knock you out, so instead, he attempts to defy and disengage you. The enemy wants to wear you down so you will lose heart and give up the fight. But here's the deal—the stakes in your fight aren't for a multimillion dollar purse and a championship belt. No. They're much higher. It's a fight for your soul, your life, your family, and for everything you hold dear.

After eight rounds of punches and jeers from Sugar Ray Leonard, the champion inside Roberto Duran died. He lost the vision of who he was and quit the fight even if that meant forfeiting the title. But guess what? After disengaging from the fight for some nine years, in the face of heavy criticism and doubt, Duran made an astonishing comeback to win the World Boxing Council world title! He chose to get back into the fight! Duran wound up as one the few boxers who continued to fight with great success into his fifties.

To be the effective warrior God destined you to be, you can't afford to lose sight of who you really are in Christ—a champion, a conqueror. Romans 8:37 declares that we are not just conquerors, but we are *more than conquerors through Him who loves us!*

You may be a wounded warrior. You're still in the fight, but staggering. If that's you, it's time to get your feet planted, your eyes refocused, and attack. If you're disengaged from the fight and are on the verge of giving up, then it's time to climb back into the ring! God wants to empower you for your comeback. But you must be intentional. Anything in life with lasting value you'll have to fight for. Nehemiah 4:14 urges us to "...*Remember the Lord, great and awesome, and fight for your brethren, your sons, your daughters, your wives, and your houses."*

In this spiritual fight you are either advancing or retreating! There is no neutral. God wants you to engage and He's the ultimate trainer. God is our *rock* and it is He who *trains our hands for war, and our fingers for battle.* It's a spiritual war that affects the physical realm. God wants to IGNITE your faith! And that's what this devotional is all about. As long as you're still breathing, it's not too late to win! So get back in the fight and finish strong!

SEEING CLEARLY

To see a man beaten, not by a better opponent, but by himself, is a tragedy.
—Cus D'Amato, Legendary Boxing Trainer

Virtually every man I have ever met doesn't really believe that God loves him. When the eyes of your heart see how deeply God loves you, it's a game changer. —Tim Clinton

You are all sons of God through faith in Christ Jesus, for all of you who were baptized into Christ have clothed yourselves with Christ (Galatians 3:26-27 NASB).

"For I know the plans I have for you," declares the Lord, *"plans to prosper you and not to harm you, plans to give you hope and a future"* (Jeremiah 29:11 NIV).

Day 1

TIME TO STEP UP

...who is this uncircumcised Philistine, that he should defy the armies of the living God? (1 Samuel 17:26).

...all progress depends on the unreasonable man. —MALCOLM GLADWELL[1]

I'm out of breath. This race is unbelievable, a race everybody wants to win.
—RICK HENDRICK, Owner, American NASCAR Team Hendrick Motorsports

The epic battle of the ages.

Everything at stake.

The future of a nation threatened—its wives, children, brethren—freedom or slavery, life or death.

Would anyone step up? Anyone?

The king didn't step up, nor did any of his valiant soldiers or decorated leaders. They were too busy trembling in their boots, paralyzed with fear—a whole army shut down.

If not for *one* young man.

Thankfully, *someone* had the guts to step up, make the call, and make a move—*one* unreasonable young man. It's amazing how just one guy who gets some crazy on can be a game changer, even if he is only a shepherd boy.

You remember the story.

Samuel the prophet was sent by God to anoint one of Jesse's sons as the next king of Israel. King Saul had disobeyed God one too many times. Now God told the prophet Samuel that He had picked one of Jesse's sons to take Saul's place. God's like that. No matter how bad things get, He's always got *some man, somewhere,* who's waiting for his time to step up.

One by one, from the oldest on down, Jesse paraded his boys by Samuel, but God said "no" to each of them. Puzzled, Samuel asked if there were any others. "Well," Jesse said, "there is my youngest, David, but he's just a shepherd boy off in the fields tending sheep." The implication: don't waste your time on him. Surely he's not the one. Jesse just didn't get it. David, in his mind, was too young, too small, too inexperienced in battle. "Go get him!" Samuel demanded. "I'll wait!" God had told the prophet:

> *Do not look at his appearance or at his physical stature.... For the Lord does not see as man sees; for man looks at the outward appearance, but the Lord looks at the heart* (1 Samuel 16:7).

When Samuel saw David, the Spirit of the Lord said, *"Arise, anoint him, for this is the one!"* (1 Sam. 16:12). David was small and ruddy on the outside, but God knew that on the inside he possessed the *heart* of a warrior. Though it wasn't time for him to take the throne, *"the Spirit of the Lord came upon David from that day forward"* (1 Sam. 16:13).

Sometime later after his anointing, David was still faithfully tending sheep, waiting, when his dad instructed him to pack some food and take it to his brothers who were on the battlefield (see 1 Sam. 17:17). These were the guys David looked up to, his heroes. You may be a man who is anointed for a certain task, but God has you in waiting until your time. Don't despise the time God has you in training, but be ready to make a move when your time comes. You've heard the saying, "It's amazing how much work, time, and effort it took to become an overnight success."

When David finally arrives at the battlefield, he's stunned by what's going on. A giant Philistine warrior-leader named Goliath is mocking, humiliating, talking smack, and threatening God's army. The ultimate trash talker, Goliath was 9 feet 6 inches tall, a monster covered in armor. Dreadfully afraid, the whole army of Israel was in flight mode. David was aghast at his brothers. He couldn't believe what he was seeing. Now we are going to find out why David was chosen to be king. He may have been small in stature but he believed in a big God who had his back.

A holy boldness rose up inside him: *"Then David spoke to the men who stood by him, saying, '...For who is this uncircumcised Philistine, that he should defy the armies of the living God?'"* (1 Sam. 17:26). In other words, "Let me at him!"

There were seeds inside David that angered him as a man. He'd seen God at work and he believed God. His brothers tried to talk him out of his insane thinking. "Go back and tend the sheep," they told him, but David didn't back down. Frustrated at his brothers for their spinelessness, he shouted, *Is there not a cause—is there not something to fight for? There's a battle to be won!*" It's easy to lose heart when the enemy is defying you and making fun, disdaining you and more. But David believed. He knew what the Lord could do. Back in the fields God had given him the strength to defeat a lion and a bear with his hands (see 1 Sam. 17:34-35). He'd become quite effective at slinging stones.

Fear, by the way, makes you play small, to pull in. Ozzie Smith said, "Show me a guy who is afraid of looking bad and I can beat him every time."[2] David had confidence of who God was in his life and who he was as a man. Even if nobody else saw it, he did.

Saul tried to give him his armor. David put it on, but it only weighed him down (see 1 Sam. 17:38-39). He said, "Nope. This isn't mine—doesn't work for me. I'm going with what God has given to me." So he packs up his sling and some stones.

Get back to the fundamentals. Remember this, separation is in the preparation and God prepares each of us uniquely. You've got gifts and talents and abilities. Maybe you've lost sight of that. To get back in the fight, you need to go back and work on your core stuff. Get back to the stuff that you know matters, the stuff that stabilizes you.

Spend time with God and the people who matter most. Pour into your life the seeds of truth and hope.

David's core came from spending time with God in the field. He knew his weapons (they had been tested). When life gets tough, when you're facing a giant, get ready. Your giant will challenge everything about you. It might even feel overwhelming. Put your faith and confidence in God like David did. He even talked smack right back to the enemy! He shouted to the giant Philistine:

> ...*You come to me with a sword, with a spear, and with a javelin. But I come to you in the name of the Lord of hosts! ...This day the Lord will deliver you into my hand, and I will strike you and take your head from you...that all the earth may know that there is a God in Israel!* (1 Samuel 17:45-46)

David knew what mattered in life. When it was his time to take the stage, he literally ran toward Goliath.

> ...*David hurried and ran toward the army to meet the Philistine. Then David put his hand in his bag and took out a stone; and he slung it and struck the Philistine in his forehead, so that the stone sank into his forehead, and he fell on his face to the earth. ...And when the Philistines saw that their champion was dead, they fled. Now the men of Israel and Judah arose and shouted, and pursued the Philistines as far as the entrance of the valley...* (1 Samuel 17:48-52).

Life is not easy. Sometimes it can feel like there is no hope. Believe that God is with you. Get some fight, some passion back in you. Go with the heart and gifts God has placed in you. It's time to step up.

Run to the battle.

Get your swagger back.

When you do, you'll pick up momentum and others will follow you. It's time for a new generation of Davids who are willing to get some fight into them. Willing to step up and do what needs to be done.

Its time to separate and consecrate yourself for battle.

You play and fight like you practice. What are you doing to get yourself ready? That's what this devotional is all about. It's about helping to anchor your faith so at the end of it all you can look back and know that you left it all on the battlefield.

PRAYER TO IGNITE

Lord, empower me to step up.

ENDNOTES

1. Malcolm Gladwell, *David and Goliath: Underdogs, Misfits, and the Art of Battling Giants* (New York: Little, Brown and Company, 2013).

2. Gary Mack, *Mind Gym: An Athlete's Guide to Inner Excellence* (New York: McGraw-Hill, 2001), 43.

Day 2

THE COURAGE TO ACT

*Be strong and very courageous. Be careful to obey
all the law my servant Moses gave you; do not turn
from it to the right or to the left, that you may be
successful wherever you go* (Joshua 1:7 NIV).

*Have I not commanded you? Be strong and
courageous. Do not be afraid; do not be discour-
aged, for the Lord your God will be with
you wherever you go* (Joshua 1:9 NIV).

*Courage is the ability to do the right thing, all the
time, no matter how painful or uncomfortable it
might be. It takes courage to say "no." It takes courage
to stand up for your convictions.* —TONY DUNGY

The term "courage" is derived from the Latin root *cor*, which
literally means heart or core. The original use of the word
"courage" meant to act according to one's core. Many Christian men know what the Holy Spirit is speaking to them
deep in the core of their being, yet there's no correspond-
ing action. Courage is all about movement toward what you
know is true. It's learned in the moment you take that first

step of faith. Sometimes courageous action means standing firm in your conviction in the face of opposition.

When considering the word "courage," often what comes to mind is some heroic act of bravery like a firefighter risking his life by running into a burning building to rescue someone. Such acts certainly take courage. Sometimes we wonder if we'd have what it takes to die as a martyr for Christ. I do believe God gives a special grace in moments like that. Dying as a martyr certainly would take incredible courage. However, it also takes courage to live for Christ, day in and day out, making hard choices with integrity. I like how D.C. Talk and The Voice of the Martyrs put it: *"You may never have to face the decision of whether or not to die for your faith, but every day you face the decision of whether or not you will live for it."* Living authentically sometimes takes more courage than dying.

For Joshua, being strong and courageous not only meant facing his fears and trusting God as he led his army into battle (see Josh. 1:9), but courage also meant walking consistently with God and being obedient to Him.

> *Be strong and very courageous. Be careful to obey all the law my servant Moses gave you; do not turn from it to the right or to the left, that you may be successful wherever you go* (Joshua 1:7 NIV).

Staying focused on God's way took courage. It also brought success.

When men live courageously, amazing things happen. Healing and hope come when we have the courage to expose our wounds to the light of God's truth and love. Families are restored. Jobs are created. Wars are won. "Give me a hundred men who fear nothing but sin, and desire nothing but God," said John Wesley, "and I will shake the world. I care not a straw whether they be clergymen or laymen; and such alone will overthrow the kingdom of Satan and build up the Kingdom of God on earth."

The apostle Paul was courageous—he even praised God in the prison dungeon after being nearly flogged to death (see Acts 16:20-25). Let's read what Paul wrote:

> And now, compelled by the Spirit, I am going to Jerusalem, not knowing what will happen to me there. I only know that in every city the Holy Spirit warns me that prison and hardships are facing me. However, I consider my life worth nothing to me; my only aim is to finish the race and complete the task the Lord Jesus has given me—the task of testifying to the good news of God's grace (Acts 20:22-24 NIV).

Let us take courage and be moved to walk in faith believing that God is a rewarder of those who diligently seek Him (see Heb. 11:6).

PRAYER TO IGNITE

Lord, thank You for giving me the courage to follow the leading of Your Spirit, regardless of the risk. May Your faithfulness give me the courage to make whatever changes, to take whatever risks, You require of me in the future.

Day 3

ONLY GOD CAN FILL THE VOID

...He [God] has also set eternity in the human heart... (Ecclesiastes 3:11 NIV).

You have made us for yourself, O God, and our hearts are restless until they find their rest in you.—SAINT AUGUSTINE[1]

King Solomon.

It's hard for us to wrap our minds around how rich he was. First Kings 10:14 tells us that Solomon received 666 talents of gold each year as a base income. In today's market that would be around $1.5 billion a year. Anyway you slice it, that's a lot of dough! Basically, Solomon was so rich, he could buy whatever he wanted, and he took full advantage of his assets. He wrote in Ecclesiastes 2:10 (NASB), *"All that my eyes desired I did not refuse them. I did not withhold my heart from any pleasure...."* Isn't that the dream of most men today? Unlimited resources? Power and respect? Excitement and pleasure? "If I could just win the lottery then I'll be all set," we secretly dream. Solomon had all of it. But listen to the next verse:

> *Thus I considered all my activities which my hands had done and the labor which I had exerted, and behold all was vanity and striving after wind and there was no profit under the sun* (Ecclesiastes 2:11 NASB).

All vanity and striving after wind? No profit? Those are some heavy duty words. But it gets worse! Solomon continued in verse 17, *"Therefore I hated life...."* Ok. Wow. So the guy who had everything—women, adventure, power, unlimited resources for his creative desires, even beautiful retreats to relieve stress—ends up hating life! Solomon didn't say he was just lacking in some area, but that he "hated life!" That's because nothing in this life can fill the void, nothing.

What was true for Solomon is true for us. There's a sin-gouged hole in the heart of every man alive—a deep void that screams to be filled. Look around at how we attempt to fill that void with everything from adrenalin-rushing activities to relationships to careers—sports cars, football, four wheelers, boats, hunting, fishing, you name it. Fun...for a while. But none of it will ultimately satisfy.

Whatever it is, whatever you are chasing will leave you empty, longing for something more. It's a never-ending cycle because only God can fill the hole in our soul—the ache in every man's heart. Solomon also wrote, *"He* [God] *has also set eternity in the human heart..."* (Ecclesiastes 3:11 NIV).

Not of this world.

We were not made for this world, but for eternity, to walk in fellowship with God. C.S. Lewis put it this way, "If I find in myself a desire which no experience in this world can satisfy, the most probable explanation is that I was made for another world."[2]

According to the Bible, substituting anything else is really idolatry. When we attempt to fill the void in us with things other than God, those things become idols. All of those "other things" are not necessarily wrong in themselves. We are free to enjoy them in their proper place; but anything in our lives that gets the devotion that God alone deserves, affects our relationship with Him. Because of our insecurities, emotional vulnerability, and longing to be needed, many of us are drawn into over-involved relationships, placing people on the throne of our lives, and in effect, making them our God. Remember, people will always fall short. Only in an ongoing relationship with God will we find the ultimate peace, intimacy, forgiveness, and joy our hearts long for.

We may think we are obeying the command of First John 5:21, *"Dear children, keep yourselves from idols"* because we don't have any statues in our homes, but we must realize that idols are more than the Israelites' golden calf. Anything that becomes our reason for living—our motivation for behavior, our "relational fuel" other than God—is an idol.

Blaise Pascal said, "There is a God-shaped vacuum in the heart of every man which cannot be filled by any created thing, but only by God, the Creator, made known through Jesus."[3]

PRAYER TO IGNITE

Lord, I recognize that only You can satisfy me. Help me to identify any idols in my life and lay them at the feet of the Cross. Fill me with Your peace, Your contentment, Yourself. Draw me to You.

ENDNOTES

1. Saint Augustine, *Confessions* (New York: Penguin, 1961), 120.
2. C.S. Lewis, *Mere Christianity* (New York: Simon & Schuster, Touchtone edition, 1996).
3. Paraphrase of Blaise Pascal, *Pensees* (New York: Penguin, 1997), 45.

Day 4

WHO'S PURSUING WHO?

For God is working in you, giving you the desire to obey him and the power to do what pleases him (Philippians 2:13 NLT).

After each failure, ask forgiveness, pick yourself up, and try again. Very often what God first helps us towards is not the virtue itself but just this power of always trying again.... We learn, on the one hand, that we cannot trust ourselves even in our best moments, and, on the other, that we need not despair even in our worst, for our failures are forgiven. The only fatal thing is to sit down content with anything less than perfection. —C.S. LEWIS[1]

Something good is happening right in the middle of the challenge or mess you find yourself in.

The truth is still true. *"God is working in you"* even if you've slipped and fallen. You may not feel it, or know it, but He's in the midst of it. He's calling your name: *"If you leave God's paths and go astray, you will hear a voice behind you say, 'No, this is the way; walk here'"* (Isaiah 30:21 TLB). That desire you have deep in your gut to fight despite yet another battle, that's the Spirit of God drawing you in. You're His child and like a loving parent His hands are cupped to his mouth and He's calling out to you from the front porch of His heart. "Son, I'm here in the midst of it with you. You *will* get through this. It's time to get back in the fight."

Jesus said, *"No man can come to me, except the Father which hath sent me draw him"* (John 6:44 KJV). If you feel that tug, be thankful. It means you're His. He knows the agony of your battle, the pain of your fight. Right in the middle of your worst living nightmare, at your lowest moment, God is still at work molding and making you. His love will never once compromise with sin, but He clings to His wounded warriors with one purpose in mind: to reclaim them—to strengthen them. "Our Lord comes to us in our weakest moment, with sin stains blotched all over our garments" writes David Wilkerson, "and He whispers, 'My strength is for you in this your hour of weakness. Don't give up. Don't panic. Don't turn away. Don't shut me out. Is there godly sorrow in you? Do you want victory? Keep moving with Me. Keep moving toward Me. My arms are still stretched out, as a mother hen spreading her wings. Come, I'll protect you from *the enemy.*'"[2]

Many times we actually begin to think we get out of our messes by pursuing God. There *is* a time when we seek Him, but the deeper truth here is that anything good that happens occurs only because of Him: *"For God is working in you, giving you the desire and the power to do what pleases him"* (Phil. 2:13 NLT). He's pursuing you! He's in your corner!

God will follow you in your rebellion, pursue you in your pain, and humble you on the mountaintop. He loves you that much. He understands your feelings of brokenness, and He loves to use powerlessness to send you fleeing back into His arms where He is waiting.

Now get up.

Climb back into the ring.

Plant your feet firmly and start swinging again.

PRAYER TO IGNITE

Thank You, Lord, for calling my name—for pursuing me. Fill me with the knowledge of who You are and Your will for my life. Work in me the desire to obey You and the power to do what pleases You.

ENDNOTES

1. C.S. Lewis, *Mere Christianity*, 94.
2. David Wilkerson, *Have You Felt Like Giving Up Lately?* (Grand Rapids, MI: Fleming H. Revell, 1960), 119.

Day 5

THE HEAD EDGE

*Sanctify them by Your truth. Your
word is truth* (John 17:17).

*The spiritual battle, the loss of victory, is always
in the thought-world.* —FRANCIS SCHAEFFER

As you advance in levels athletically, the skill gap closes. What separates those who can play at the highest levels and those who can't is mental. It's called *The Head Edge*. The baseball legend and Hall of Famer Ty Cobb quipped, "The most important part of a player's body is above his shoulders." Professional golfer Bobby Jones said, "Golf is a game that is played on a five-inch course—the distance between your ears."[1] It's true in golf and it's true in life. Those who train physically *and* mentally will out-perform those who just train physically, hands down.

In the Christian life, the great battle is for the mind. Paul urged us to *"be transformed by the renewing of your mind"* (Rom. 12:2). Why? The enemy is a liar. That's why. John 8:44 says, *"...there is no truth in him* [the devil]. *When he speaks a lie, he speaks from his own resources, for he is a liar and the father of it."*

When the battle for our minds begins, it starts with a barrage of destructive ideas, suspicions, doubts, and fears. The enemy's goal is for those lies to take root and to become strongholds in our minds that ultimately determine our actions. A stronghold can be a pattern of thinking that becomes so set in our mind that we convince ourselves it is right or true—even when it's not. It can lead us to destructive habits like addiction, self-hatred, depression, fear, and unhealthy dependence on others.

Strongholds begin as small seeds, single thoughts planted in our mind. Over time, if these seeds are not weeded out, they take root and grow into full-fledged vices that dominate us. The good news is that we don't have to live in the bondage these strongholds create. Through God's leading and renewal, we can make daily choices to "put off" our old destructive habits and "put on" new choices that become new habits (see Eph. 4:22-24).

> *For the weapons of our warfare are not carnal but mighty in God for pulling down strongholds, casting down arguments and every high thing that exalts itself against the knowledge of God, bringing every thought into captivity to the obedience of Christ* (2 Corinthians 10:4-5).

The way we demolish strongholds is by binding our thoughts and our will to the will of God through prayer. As we persistently pray in this manner, the Holy Spirit brings to our mind areas and thought patterns that do not line up with the Word of God. When these thoughts enter our minds, it is our responsibility to compare them to what we know to be true based on the Word of God. Romans 12:3 calls it a sober assessment. That's how we discern truth from falsehood and begin to renew our mind. We look to Jesus. He said, *"I am the way and the truth and the life"* (John 14:6). On the other hand, Jesus described Satan as a *"liar and the father of lies"* (John 8:44 NIV).

Strongholds bind, but truth sets free. Jesus said, *"If you abide in My word, you are My disciples indeed. And you shall know the truth, and the truth shall make you free"* (John 8:31-32). Freedom comes by immersing yourself in truth and renewing your mind. It's the *head edge*. You may be going through a time of darkness in your life. Your faith and sanity are under attack; those destructive habits may be out of control. You don't have to let the enemy destroy you or your faith. It's on the battleground of our psyche that we win or lose the fight against Satan and his system to keep us bound by strongholds. Let God's eternal truth demolish the strongholds in your life and set you free from self destruction.

Get the *head edge*.

PRAYER TO IGNITE

God, You are the source of all truth. Renew my mind and give me a discerning spirit. Help me to release the strongholds in my life, the destructive habits, and experience freedom.

ENDNOTE

1.   http://www.mentaledgesports.com/quotes/; accessed 6/2/14.

FLAWED, BUT INCREDIBLY VALUABLE

For I know that in me (that is, in my flesh)
nothing good dwells.... If anyone is in Christ,
he is a new creation; old things have passed
away; behold, all things have become new
(Romans 7:18; 2 Corinthians 5:17).

The mind of a Pharisee thinks truth is more
important than love, but Jesus showed us that
love is the most important part of truth.
—Adapted from *Don Francisco's Pharisiatis Test*[1]

Great athletes know that to separate physically from the pack, both exercise and proper nutrition go hand in hand. Focusing on only one aspect causes an unbalance. It takes both to thrive at a high level. Likewise, to become a warrior who is fully engaged in the fight, we need both truth and love. We like the love part, but truth is sometimes hard to hear. Yet, we can't grow and thrive in life unless both are active. Truth and love are a powerful combination. Our tendency in today's society is to build our self-esteem by pouring out praises; accentuating the positive, overlooking faults and imperfections. Instead of naming sin for what it really is, rebellion against God, we like to rename it to try and minimize our feelings of guilt. But sin is so serious that Jesus had to endure the Cross in order to deal with it.

The truth is that we are flawed; and even when we try to do good, we still fail. We can't overcome this problem by speaking positively or pumping up our self-esteem or pretending our flaws don't exist. This fact is not intended to result in you beating yourself up for being flawed, rather so you will grasp the truth that we are all sinners in need of Someone to rescue us because we can't rescue ourselves. We desperately need a Savior.

The good news is God understands who we are: *"As a father pities his children, so the Lord pities those who fear Him. For He knows our frame; He remembers that we are dust"* (Ps. 103:13-14).

The better news is God understands who we are and He loves us anyway! He loves us so much that He sent Jesus to pay the price of redemption that we could not possibly pay. God demonstrated *"His own love toward us, in that while we were still sinners, Christ died for us"* (Rom. 5:8). We have incredible value because God created us and died for us.

Through embracing the whole truth—that we are flawed but through Christ we are incredibly valuable—we are free to *"come boldly to the throne of grace,"* totally transparent and completely honest, to *"obtain mercy and find grace to help in our time of need"* (see Heb. 4:16).

The truth is, God *"made Him who knew no sin to be sin for us, that we might become the righteousness of God in Him"* (2 Cor. 5:21). We are right before God because of Jesus and His love for us.

> Birds need two wings to fly. With only one wing, they're grounded. The gospel flies with the wings of grace [love] and truth. Not one, but both.
>
> —RANDY ALCORN[2]

PRAYER TO IGNITE

God, thank You that my repeated failures can never drive me beyond the reach of Your love. Thank You for sending Jesus to pay the price for my sins. I acknowledge that I am flawed, but I'm also incredibly valuable.

ENDNOTES

1. Wayne Jacobsen, *He Loves Me! Learning to Live in the Father's Affection* (Newbury Park, CA: Windblown Media, 2007), 181.

2. Randy Alcorn, *The Grace and Truth Paradox* (Sisters, OR: Multnomah Books, 2002), 16.

Day 7

A CLEAN HEART

*Create in me a clean heart, O God, and renew
a steadfast spirit within me* (Psalm 51:10)

*Being a Christian is more than just an instantaneous
conversion—it is a daily process whereby you grow
to be more and more like Christ.* —BILLY GRAHAM[1]

"Lord Jesus, create a clean heart and renew a right spirit within me." When you pray that from the heart, then you're getting down to real business. Becoming the man God wants us to be involves so much more than going to church each week, serving on a ton of ministry committees, or taking part in a plethora of outreach programs. Christianity is not about going through religious motions. It's about God taking our old hearts, cleaning them, and recreating them. It's about you and God connecting on a deeper level.

Galatians 5:25 (KJV) says, *"If we live in the Spirit, let us also walk in the Spirit."* When you walk in step with the Spirit through His Word and obeying His lead, Christ's character is being formed in you. That's what creates real and lasting change. Paul's earnest goal for his disciples wasn't that they get involved in more religious activity, but that Christ was formed in them. He wrote to the Galatians, *"My little children, for whom I labor in birth again until Christ is formed in you"* (Gal. 4:19). When we ask God to create a clean heart in us, in reality, we are asking Him to make us more like Jesus.

When asked about the process of sculpting his famous statue of David, it is said that Michelangelo remarked, "I knew David was in there so I just chipped away the stone that didn't look like him." That's what the Holy Spirit does to us. As we draw into an intimate relationship with God, the Holy Spirit begins the process of chipping away the things that don't look like Jesus and then shaping us into His image. Authentic change and healing are the result. Anything else amounts to religious self-help.

When we start becoming more like Jesus, another wonderful thing happens. People begin to notice something different in us. We're not trying to be different, we just are as a result of being in His presence. Roy Hicks Jr. wrote, "Imagine a man who has been so conformed to Jesus' image that just by knowing him the people he comes in contact with every day—his wife, his children, men and women at work—discover God and their own individual potential."[2]

Become the man God has called you to be. Let Him create a clean heart in you and chip away at those things that are not like Jesus.

PRAYER TO IGNITE

God, cleanse my heart. I give You permission to chisel me into Your image. Draw me by Your Spirit into fellowship with You and let my life be a reflection of You.

ENDNOTES

1. http://www.tentmaker.org/Quotes/keys.htm; accessed 6/5/14.
2. Roy Hicks Jr., *A Small Book about God* (Sisters, OR: Multnomah Books, 1997), 42.

Day 8

HE LOVES ME ANYWAY

*O wretched man that I am! Who will deliver
me from this body of death?* (Romans 7:24)

*He knows me.... This is momentous knowledge....
There is tremendous relief in knowing that his love
to me is utterly realistic, based at every point on
prior knowledge of the worst about me, so that no
discovery now can disillusion him about me, in the
way I am so often disillusioned about myself, and
quench his determination to bless me.* —J.I. PACKER[1]

Even the great apostle Paul was aware of his own weak-
nesses. Consider this: even after the Lord Himself appeared
to Paul in a blinding light on the Damascus Road he still
struggled with his old fleshly nature. Let's read what Paul
wrote about himself:

*For we know that the law is spiritual, but I am
carnal, sold under sin. For what I am doing, I do not
understand. For what I will to do, that I do not practice; but what I hate, that I do"* (Romans 7:14-15).

Note, Paul is writing in the present tense. He doesn't say "I was" but "I am." He goes on to write, *"For I know that in me (that is, in my flesh) nothing good dwells…. For the good that I will to do, I do not do; but the evil I will not to do, that I practice"* (Rom. 7:18-19). When the full weight of Paul's dilemma bore down on him and his powerlessness to change himself, he cried out, "O wretched man that I am! Who will deliver me from this body of death?" (Rom. 7:24).

Paul's cry is the cry of all men. And it's an important cry. As much as it is unpopular in today's feel-good, politically correct society, it's imperative to see ourselves as we really are. Yes, we *are* champions in *our new nature,* yet we are still wretches in our old and in need of His constant grace. I love the following story by Randy Alcorn:

> Before I spoke at a conference, a soloist sang one of my favorite songs, "Amazing Grace." It was beautiful. Until she got to the tenth word. "Amazing grace! How sweet the sound that saved a soul like me!" My heart sank. The word wretch had been edited out! I thought about John Newton, the songwriter. This former slave trader, guilty of the vilest sins, knew he was a wretch. And that's what made God's grace so "amazing." If we're nothing more than morally neutral "souls," do you see what that does? It guts grace…When you cut wretch out of the song, you shrink grace. You reduce it to something more sensible, less surprising. If you weren't so bad without Christ, why did He have to endure the cross? Paul

said if men were good enough, then "Christ died for nothing" (Galatians 2:21).[2]

Seeing and confronting our own sinfulness should bring the same response from us that it did from Paul and John Newton—amazing grace that saved a wretch like me! Only Jesus saves us from the clutches of sin. He is our answer, not only for our initial salvation, but for our ongoing fight against our old nature that seeks to have its way with us. *"But I see another law at work in me, waging war against the law of my mind and making me a prisoner of the law of sin at work within me"* (Rom. 7:23 NIV).

You don't have to be dominated. Thankfully, Paul knew the answer to his dilemma as he breaks forth in jubilant praise! *"Thanks be to God through Jesus Christ our Lord!"* (Rom. 7:25 NASB). Jesus provides the gift of salvation and the power for continued victory when we choose to walk in the Spirit. *"I say then: Walk in the Spirit, and you shall not fulfill the lust of the flesh. But if you are led by the Spirit, you are not under the law"* (Gal. 5:16,18).

Speaking of this battle with our flesh, C.S. Lewis summed it up well:

> It cures our illusions about ourselves and teaches us to depend on God. We learn, on the one hand, that we cannot trust ourselves even in our best moments and on the other we need not despair in our worst for our failures are forgiven. The only fatal thing is to sit down content with anything less than perfection."[3]

No matter how many times you've been knocked down, keep getting up and stay in the fight. Don't quit.

PRAYER TO IGNITE

Thank You, Jesus, that You saved me from my wretchedness. You are my only hope, and I lean desperately and completely on You. Give me the strength to keep bringing my sins to You and to keep getting back up.

ENDNOTES

1.   J.I. Packer *Knowing God* (Downers Grove, IL: InterVarsity Press, 1993), 41-42, emphasis added.

2.   Randy Alcorn, *The Grace and Truth Paradox* (Sisters, OR: Multnomah Books, 2003), 31.

3.   C.S. Lewis, *Mere Christianity*, 94.

PRACTICE MAKES PERMANENT

...train yourself for godliness (1 Timothy 4:7 ESV).

*We cannot attain or earn this righteousness...
it is a grace that is given.... The Disciplines
allow us to place ourselves before God so that
he can transform us.* —RICHARD FOSTER[1]

The shortstop made a crazy play, flipping the ball to the second baseman who rifled it to first. A perfect double play to end what could have been a disastrous inning. Someone sitting in the stands commented on how these 17-year-old boys made the play look easy. One of the dads who helped coach responded, "That's because they've practiced that play thousands of times! It's become second nature to them."

It's been said, "Practice makes perfect." That is not entirely true. Practice makes *permanent*. Do it over and over again incorrectly, and you have simply developed a bad habit. "Perfect practice makes perfect." It takes a lot of sacrifice—blood, sweat, and guts—to achieve excellence, to separate yourself.

The apostle Paul understood that this same degree of intensity was necessary to reach a level of "spiritual" excellence. In his letter to young Timothy, Paul urges him to *"train yourself for godliness"* (1 Tim. 4:7 ESV). It's interesting that the Greek word for "train" is *gymnazo,* from which we get the word gymnasium, and it means to exercise vigorously. Paul uses the word "train" to denote strenuous spiritual exercise in order to produce godliness. He goes on to say, *"... godliness is of value in every way, as it holds promise for the present life and also for the life to come"* (1 Tim. 4:8 ESV).

Promise for the life to come—but also for *this* present life. Too often in this world our spiritual lives are lethargic and weak. Maybe our lack of power as Christians is simply spiritual *inactivity.* Maybe we need to get our fight back. Get back in the Word. Seek spiritual excellence in prayer. Inspiration comes by perspiration.

Paul must have known that there would be a temptation for Timothy to be lackadaisical in his day-to-day journey. Paul reminded him, *"Do not neglect the spiritual gift within you..."* (1 Tim. 4:14 NASB). *"For to this end we toil and strive..."* (1 Tim. 4:10 ESV). *"Practice these things, immerse yourself in them..."* (1 Tim. 4:15 ESV).

A.W. Tozer said, "We must face the fact that many today are notoriously careless in their living. This attitude finds its way into the church. We have liberty, we have money, we live in comparative luxury. As a result, discipline practically has disappeared."

Spiritual determination.

Sacred vigorous exercise.

Daily devotional discipline.

It's all part of your championship training regimen.

PRAYER TO IGNITE

God, help me get back in the fight and to train rigorously like a champion. I know You have great things in store for me and the ones I love.

ENDNOTE

1. Richard Foster, *Celebration of Discipline* (San Francisco: HarperCollins, 1978), 6-7.

Day 10

A VERY REAL OPPONENT

For we wrestle not against flesh and blood, but
against principalities, against powers, against the
rulers of the darkness of this world, against spiritual
wickedness in high places (Ephesians 6:12 KJV).

You were rubbed with oil like an athlete—
Christ's athlete—as though in preparation for
an earthly wrestling match, and you agreed to
take on your opponent. —AMBROSE OF MILAN[1]

Jesus was God in the flesh; and make no mistake about it, He believed in evil and Satan, the prince and power of the air. Jesus referred to Satan twenty-five times. He also dealt with demons on a regular basis. When tempted in the desert for forty days, Jesus didn't appeal to mind over matter or positive thinking to resist the temptation. He instead recognized the source of His temptation:

Then Jesus said to him, "Away with you, Satan!
For it is written, 'You shall worship the Lord your

God, and Him only you shall serve'" (Matthew 4:10).

When Jesus told the parable of the sower, He compared the seed to the Word of God and the soil to our hearts. He said:

> *The sower sows the word. And these are the ones by the wayside where the word is sown. When they hear, Satan comes immediately and takes away the word that was sown in their hearts* (Mark 4:14-15).

If you have any value to God, all hell will be against you. C.H. Spurgeon warned:

> There is nothing which Satan can do for his evil cause which he does not do. We may be half-hearted, but he never is. He is the very image of ceaseless industry and indefatigable earnestness. He will do all that can be done in the time of his permitted range. We may be sure that he will never lose a day.[2]

Jesus warned Peter, "*Simon, Simon! Indeed, Satan has asked for you, that he may sift you as wheat*" (Luke 22:31). Likewise, the apostle Paul warned us to stay alert *"in order that Satan might not outwit us. For we are not unaware of his schemes"* (2 Cor. 2:11 NIV). Did you get that? The evil one has schemes and is trying to outwit us. We must never forget that there is an actual enemy with a legion of demonic troops that controls this world system and is working behind the scenes to defeat us. It's real. There are unseen battles continually taking place all around us.

Ephesians 6:12 (KJV) makes it clear that the war is real and certainly relevant:

> *For we wrestle not against flesh and blood, but against principalities, against powers, against the rulers of the darkness of this world, against spiritual wickedness in high places.*

Our struggle in life is in part due to a wrestling match with spiritual forces, and the primary way that demonic forces attack us is through our minds. Those who win this fight and experience victory must diligently protect their minds by putting on the full armor of God: *"Finally, be strong in the Lord and in his mighty power. Put on the full armor of God, so that you can take your stand against the devil's schemes"* (Eph. 6:10-11 NIV).

God's armor (see Eph. 6:13-17) is the *helmet of salvation* to protect your mind by holding the thoughts of God's purpose for your life and taking captive every thought to the obedience of Christ. The *breastplate of righteousness* to keep your heart safe and pure by reading the Word of God and letting the Holy Spirit breathe life and meaning into His words. Having our *feet shod with the preparation of the gospel of peace* is to stand firm in your beliefs and to always be prepared to share the gospel. The *belt of truth* is to walk with integrity and speak the truth in love. You take the *shield of faith* to extinguish the fiery darts of the enemy. You tell God, "My faith is in You, Lord, I believe in You. I believe that by speaking the Word of God I have divine power over the lies of the enemy." The *sword of the Spirit* that is the Word of God. "God, I acknowledge that Your Word is alive and powerful, penetrating the innermost parts of my person even my thoughts and intents."

This fight we are in is very real and we have a full arsenal of armor to equip us. Through the power of God's Word and perseverance in prayer we can stand firm and trust God to see us through.

PRAYER TO IGNITE

God, I put on the whole armor of God so I can stand against the enemy. I believe in the power of Your Word. I set my mind on You. Help me stay alert and remain steadfast as I engage in the fight of my life.

ENDNOTES

1.   Chip Ingram, *The Invisible War, What Every Believer Needs to Know about Satan, Demons, and Spiritual Warfare* (Grand Rapids, MI: Baker Books, 2006), 65.

2.   C.H. Spurgeon, "Satan in a Rage," Sermon #1502. Delivered November 2, 1879, at the Metropolitan Tabernacle, Newington. http://www.spurgeongems.org/vols25-27/chs1502.pdf; accessed 6/3/14.

Day II

MIND GAMES

*For the weapons of our warfare are not carnal
but mighty in God for pulling down strongholds,
casting down arguments and every high thing
that exalts itself against the knowledge of God,
bringing every thought into captivity to the
obedience of Christ (2 Corinthians 10:4-5).*

*To renew your mind is to involve yourself in the
process of allowing God to bring to the surface
the lies you have mistakenly accepted and replace
them with truth.* —CHARLES STANLEY

Crazy thoughts...we all have them from time to time.

Consuming thoughts...those are the ones that won't
be denied.

Unrelenting thoughts...that won't let you sleep.

Private thoughts...that stubbornly fuel emotions of lust,
anger, fear, sorrow, and even hopelessness.

Infected thoughts...that are often destructive in relationships with those closest to us, even our relationship
with God.

Even the psalmist struggled with *"Anxious thoughts* [that] *multiply within me..."* (Ps. 94:19 NASB). The scary part is when we start believing them! *"For as he thinks within himself, so is he"* (Prov. 23:7 NASB).

The antidote?

> *Finally, brothers, whatever is true, whatever is honorable, whatever is just, whatever is pure, whatever is lovely, whatever is commendable, if there is any excellence, if there is anything worthy of praise, think about these things* (Philippians 4:8 ESV).

That's a bunch of "whatevers" to think about.

What you fill your mind with will largely determine what type of thoughts you have. You've heard the old saying, "Garbage in, garbage out." It's true.

And there is a challenge; the evil one, known as the "father of lies," constantly bombards our minds. And his mind games become a battlefield—a boxing ring. Paul said we should take *"every thought captive to the obedience of Christ"* (2 Cor. 10:5 NASB). That means grabbing that thought the second it pops up and speaking the truth of God's Word to it. Knowing it and doing it are two different things.

Speaking of war, when Paul delineates and lists the *"full armor of God"* used to *"stand firm against the schemes of the devil"* in Ephesians 6, he only records one *offensive weapon*: *"And take...the sword of the Spirit, which is the word of God"* (Eph. 6:17 NASB).

When the enemy, Satan, came against Jesus in the wilderness, Jesus countered the onslaught by saying, *"It is written."*

The spiritual weapon given to us by the Lord, to battle the formation of these debilitating and controlling thoughts, is God's Word. In Ephesians 5:26 (ESV), Paul says that Christ sanctifies and cleanses the body of Christ *"by the washing of water by the word."* Our thought life can, and will be washed clean by soaking and meditating in His written Word. As you do this, *"the peace of God, which surpasses all understanding, will guard your hearts and your minds in Christ Jesus"* (Phil. 4:7 ESV).

PRAYER TO IGNITE

Lord, fill my mind with Your truth and wash me with Your Word. Empower me to cast down vain imaginings and every thought that rises up against You in my mind.

TRAINING

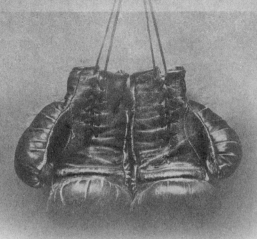

*The fight is won or lost far away from witnesses—
behind the lines, in the gym and out there
on the road [running], long before I dance
under those lights.* —MUHAMMAD ALI

*It's not the will to win that matters—everyone
has that. It's the will to prepare to win that
matters.* —PAUL "BEAR" BRYANT

*But [like a boxer] I buffet my body [handle it
roughly, discipline it by hardships] and subdue it,
for fear that after proclaiming to others the Gospel
and things pertaining to it, I myself should become
unfit [not stand the test, be unapproved and rejected
as a counterfeit]* (1 Corinthians 9:27 AMP).

Day 12

FROM DISAPPOINTMENT TO REAPPOINTMENT

He said to him the third time, "Simon, son of Jonah, do you love me?" Peter was grieved because he said to him the third time, "Do you love me?" And he said to him, "Lord, you know all things; you know that I love you." Jesus said to him, "Feed my sheep" (John 21:17 ESV).

The lows are disappointing but that makes the high much sweeter, that's what drives me. —Tim Tebow

Sometimes the crystal bowl of life is not just broken, it's shattered, completely ruined, and beyond repair. Barring a miracle, our frantic efforts to fix it will be a waste of time and energy. Life often leaves us in irreparable situations. When this happens we experience a wide array of emotions ranging from anger and loss to emptiness and disappointment.

You may have been climbing the company ladder when you suddenly found yourself on the wrong end of corporate downsizing. Perhaps you were an athlete, giving your all, when you blew out a knee, dashing your chances for that athletic scholarship. Or maybe your ex-wife has moved on with life and is remarried, but you had been hanging on to hope for reconciliation. Whatever the reason, you may now find yourself having to deal with disabling disappointment and perhaps even despair. If so, there is a solution for your situation. Often our faith is reinforced right in the middle of disappointment.

Disappointments are an inevitable part of life, but even these letdowns can produce positive results. God may be using them to reinvent you. This is exactly the business God is in—the business of turning disappointments into reappointments. Sometimes closed doors, failure, and disappointment can become the greatest avenues to blessings.

Because of his own failure, Peter was more than a little disappointed. He was devastated, crushed, and humiliated. After faithfully following Jesus for more than three years, Peter, in a moment of weakness and cowardice, denied Him—just as Jesus had predicted—not once, but three times! (See Mark 14:72.) And once Jesus had been crucified, Peter felt as if his life were over, that there was nothing left to live for. The only solution was to hide out, wallow in his depression, and try to figure out what to do with the mess he'd made of his life.

Then something happened: the resurrection. When Peter came face-to-face with the risen Christ, another miracle happened. Peter the denier became Peter the apostle. Christ forgave him, healed him, and reappointed him to something greater! On the shores of the Sea of Galilee, Jesus gave Peter a new assignment.

So when they had eaten breakfast, Jesus said to Simon Peter, "Simon, son of Jonah, do you love Me more than these?"

He said to Him, "Yes, Lord; You know that I love You."

He said to him, "Feed My lambs."

He said to him again a second time, "Simon, son of Jonah, do you love Me?"

He said to Him, "Yes, Lord; You know that I love You."

He said to him, "Tend My sheep."

He said to him the third time, "Simon, son of Jonah, do you love Me?" Peter was grieved because He said to him the third time, "Do you love Me?"

And he said to Him, "Lord, You know all things; You know that I love You."

Jesus said to him, "Feed My sheep" (John 21:15-17).

The rest of the story is that Peter accepted his new assignment and became a pillar of the early church that transformed the face of the earth. Just as He did with Peter, whenever we allow the risen Christ to touch our areas of profound disappointment, He will reappoint us to something greater.

PRAYER TO IGNITE

God, I choose to trust that as I surrender my disappointments to You, You will turn them into reappointments.

Day 13

EARTHQUAKE PRAISE

*Rejoice in the Lord always. Again I will
say, rejoice!* (Philippians 4:4)

*Many Christians have made the dramatic discovery
of the ancient truth that we are called to praise
God in all circumstances, and that miracles are
often the result, the biggest of all usually being
the melting of our heart.* —JUDSON CORNWALL

The apostle Paul wasn't trying to sound religious when he encouraged us to rejoice in the Lord always. I think he had a pretty good idea of what "always" meant. He'd been shipwrecked, beaten several times, left for dead, abandoned by friends, and imprisoned. Not to mention, he had that annoying little thorn in the flesh that just wouldn't go away no matter how much he prayed. Paul knew pain. He knew adversity. Yet, he also knew a real God, a God who never promised to keep us from suffering but promised to be with us in our suffering.

Paul understood that praise freed his spirit and released his faith. I'm sure you remember the time he and his companion, Silas, were cast into prison. Try to picture that day. The marketplace was bustling with activity as the Middle Eastern sun of Macedonia bore down on them, amplifying the mingled smell of body odor, animals, leather, and produce. The crowd parted and formed a huge circle around Paul and Silas as they were dragged naked through the street and then flogged.

The iron pellets tied to the ends of the leather whips actually shattered bones as they landed across their backs. With each crack of the whip, the crowd cheered. Some spat upon their blood-covered bodies. Finally, when Paul and Silas lay face down in the dirt, the jailers dragged them away. When Paul and Silas were carried to prison, they didn't know what the future held. They had zero reason to believe that they would ever see the light of day again. Yet what do we see?

Again and again the rods slashed down across their bared backs; and afterwards they were thrown into prison. The jailer was threatened with death if they escaped, so he took no chances, but put them into the inner dungeon and clamped their feet into the stocks. Around midnight, as Paul and Silas were praying and singing hymns to the Lord—and the other prisoners were listening— suddenly there was a great earthquake; the prison was shaken to its foundations, all the doors flew open—and the chains of every prisoner fell off! (Acts 16:23-26 TLB)

Authentic praise is when we extol the character and faithfulness of God even when we don't understand the circumstances around us. It's affirming that He's in control. Earthquake praise happens when we choose to praise God smack-dab in the middle of the darkest, filthiest dungeons of life, when we are chained down, with seemingly no way out. Praise is a key that can fling open the door to victory in our lives.

PRAYER TO IGNITE

God, we offer You the sacrifice of praise and thanksgiving. Let us be molded into Your image as we go through times of pain and suffering.

Day 14

CHOICES

...choose this day whom you will serve....
But as for me and my house we will
serve the Lord (Joshua 24:15 ESV).

God develops the fruit of the Spirit in your life
by allowing you to experience circumstances
in which you're tempted to express the exact
opposite quality. Character development always
involves a choice, and temptation provides
that opportunity. —RICK WARREN[1]

Choices.

You *are* your choices.

Show me your friends, I'll show you your future.

Show me your diet and exercise patterns, I'll show you your health.

Show me your checkbook, I'll show you your heart.

We make choices about how to spend our time.

There are 86,400 seconds in a day.

How much time goes to our kids, our wife...God?

Life is all about choices.

Each day you make choices by what you do or don't do, choices that largely determine what kind of day we will have—and even some that affect the course of our lives. I love how author Tim Keller put it, "Every choice we make is a part of God's plan for our life—and we are responsible for every choice we make."[2] Because many of the conscious choices we make carry with them eternal consequences, we must choose wisely. John Chrysostom said it this way, "God, having placed good and evil in our power, has given us full freedom of choice...."[3]

Recently as I was reading Psalm 119, two particular "choosing" verses caught my attention:

> *I have chosen the way of faithfulness; I set your rules before me* (Psalm 119:30 ESV).

> *Let your hand be ready to help me, for I have chosen your precepts* (Psalm 119:173 ESV).

What's interesting is that in Hebrew, the word "chosen" means to *select what is the better part of a thing—something you delight in*. The psalmist is consciously choosing to live a life of faithfulness to the Lord, as well as declaring that he has continuously chosen the precepts (the commandments and words) of the Lord because he understood that these choices were the best part of life—the part he delighted in.

Think about that. Are our daily choices made in light of being faithful and in accordance with God's Word? When given "free" time during the day, what do we choose to do with it? Do we delight in acts of faithfulness that line up with His precepts? We experience unbroken union and communion with Jesus when we make deliberate choices to spend time alone with Him each day.

It has been said that what a man or woman chooses to do when they are totally alone—when no one will see—or knows—that is who they truly are.

We might do well to be reminded again of the admonition of Joshua to the children of Israel as his life was drawing to a close, "...*choose this day whom you will serve...*" to which he added this declaration, "*But as for me and my house we will serve the Lord*" (Joshua 24:15 ESV).

As a man, we choose to stay in the fight. One of the life-altering precepts about life in Christ is that every day you have the opportunity to make new choices. God-given opportunities to choose faithfulness—to choose His Word and His ways.

Choose those things which are best.

PRAYER TO IGNITE

Lord, today I choose You.

ENDNOTES

1.   Rick Warren, *The Purpose Driven Life* (Grand Rapids, MI: Zondervan, 2002), 202.
2.   Timothy Keller, *Every Good Endeavor: Connecting Your Work to God's Work* (New York: Penguin Group, 2012).
3.   John Chrysostom, Institutes of the Christian Religion.

Day 15

THE SECRET PLACE

*But when you pray, go into your room and
shut the door and pray to your Father who
is in secret...* (Matthew 6:6 ESV).

*Therefore, whether the desire for prayer is on
you or not, get to your closet at the set time;
shut yourself in with God; wait upon Him; seek
His face; realize Him; pray.* —R.F. HORTON

Where do you live?

Where do you sleep?

Where do you eat?

When and *where* do you pray?

Most would respond to "When and where do you pray?"
with the following answers: "Over food," "With my kids,"
"In church." Common answers. Good answers.

But Jesus talked about a place of prayer that really mattered to Him—the "secret place." A place of solitude where
He would often withdraw into privacy and spiritual intimacy with His Father.

It is interesting that Jesus used the religious hypocrites of His day as a warning about prayer. They loved to pray in public. For show. With loud voices. Out of duty and pride. Jesus made it clear that *being seen by others was their reward* (see Matt. 6:5 ESV).

With encouraging direction Jesus continues, *"But when you pray, go into your room and shut the door and pray to your Father who is in secret..."* (Matt. 6:6 ESV).

The "secret place." Where God abides. Where He sees into our hearts and minds. The room in which God is in touch with the things we think go unnoticed, but that matter deeply to Him and us.

And by the way, Jesus added, *"your Father who sees in secret will reward you"* (Matt. 6:6 ESV). Sowing in the secret place of prayer, reaps God's rewards.

You can tell those people who pray in secret. Their countenance shines with the very glory of God. They have a humble boldness. A gentle strength. A quiet confidence. The mind of Christ.

But too often the pace of life has paralyzed the power of our prayers. We have relegated our "quiet time" to spiritual fast food, microwaved on the fly. A quick "Bless me Lord" as we head off to bed or into a day of the unknown.

Finding time to pray, much less a "secret place" is hard to do with the press of the world, and the pressures of our much-too-busy lives.

Jesus understood this. When the *"great crowds gathered to hear him* [Jesus] *and to be healed of their infirmities"*

(Luke 5:15 ESV), there was the potential for His life to become frantic and a bit chaotic. Luke 5:16 says that it was at those times Jesus *"would withdraw to desolate places and pray."*

In the very next chapter of Luke, when the religious leaders were *"filled with fury"* and began to conspire about how to kill Jesus, *"he went out to the mountain to pray, and all night he continued in prayer to God"* (Luke 6:10-12 ESV).

The "secret place." The back side of the mountain. The woods. Your favorite fishing spot, or your Man Cave. The space in life where it's just you and God. It is private. Separate. Alone. No show and tell there. No flowery words meant to impress. Just raw, direct intimacy with your Creator.

In the secret place, it's God and you.

Make *a room* for God in your life; a secret place where you *"worship the Lord in the splendor of holiness"* (Ps. 29:2 ESV).

PRAYER TO IGNITE

God, help me find that secret place where I can push aside the press of the day. Where it's just You and me. I worship and praise Your holy name.

Day 16

WHATEVER HE SAYS

His mother said to the servants, "Whatever
He says to you, do it" (John 2:5).

Unless he obeys, a man cannot believe.
—DIETRICH BONHOEFFER

Jesus, his mother, and disciples, were attending a wedding in Galilee when the wine ran out. Not good. Someone had seriously messed up. The Bible identifies that person as the "Master of the feast." Today he'd be called the "Wedding Planner." In that culture, such a miscalculation would have totally humiliated the bride and groom. Back then, you couldn't just send a gopher down to the local Wal-Mart. When you were out, that was it. They could serve water, but who wants to drink water at a wedding? The servants must've been freaking out because when Mary saw their dilemma, she immediately looked to her Son and said, *"They have no wine"* (John 2:3). But she said it with an inference like, "Jesus—*they have no wine*—do something!" Or, *"They have no wine*—can you please help these poor people out?"

Even though it wasn't Jesus' time to make His ministry public and He let his mother know it (see John 2:4), Mary knew who Jesus was. She knew His character. She knew He was more than just her son. Boldly, and without hesitation, Mary directed the servants to Jesus and told them, *"Whatever He says to you, do it"* (John 2:5). The implication was that no matter what Jesus instructs you to do, even if you don't understand it, even if you can't see the outcome—do it anyway!

Surprisingly, despite His initial reluctance, Jesus obliges His mother. Mothers have that kind of influence! He told the servants to fill the six empty water pots to the brim with water. Now just think about this for a moment. These water pots held twenty to thirty gallons each. They were the size of trashcans! With no running water or hosepipes to stretch out, it took considerable labor to fill them. The pots had to be carried to the water source, which was probably a considerable distance away. Thirty gallons of water weighs over 250 pounds. Add to that the weight of the pot itself and you're looking at 300 pounds. It had to have taken at least two servants on each pot to tote them back. I can only imagine the rolling of eyes and bewildered looks the servants gave each other while they were filling and toting those jars. I would have loved to be a fly on one of those pots.

Then, after getting back to the wedding, Jesus tells them to dip the water and take some to the master of the feast who was most likely hyperventilating because the wine was out. Imagine that. Imagine the risk, *"I'm dipping out water here and taking it to my boss as if it's wine. How crazy is that? We are going to look like fools! We're getting fired!"* Remember, there's no record that Jesus had ever done a public miracle before and He didn't tell them what the outcome was going to be. Yet one of the amazing parts of this story is that they obeyed!

Here's the question. What's He saying to *you*? Are *you* willing to obey? To do whatever Jesus says even when He doesn't tell you what the outcome is going to be?

Do what He says in your personal life.

Do what He says in your home, in your family.

Do what He says in the place where you work.

Think about it.

Henry Blackaby wrote, "If you know that God loves you, you should never question a directive from Him. It will always be right and best. When He gives you a directive, you are not just to observe it, discuss it, or debate it. You are to obey it."[1]

PRAYER TO IGNITE

Lord, help me to hear Your voice and obey. When I struggle with not understanding or knowing the outcome, strengthen me to trust You no matter what.

ENDNOTE

1.   Henry T. Blackaby, Claude V. King, *Experiencing God: Knowing and Doing the Will of God* (Nashville: TN, Broadman & Holman Publishers, 1994), 148.

Day 17

IF I JUST KNEW WHAT TO DO

*If you leave God's paths and go astray, you
will hear a voice behind you say, "No, this is
the way; walk here (Isaiah 30:21 TLB).*

*But the Helper, the Holy Spirit, whom
the Father will send in My name, He will
teach you all things... (John 14:26).*

*If you were to do everything that Jesus tells
you one day at a time, you always would
be right in the center of where God wants
you to be.* —HENRY T. BLACKABY[1]

After the previous devotion about "doing whatever Jesus
says," you may be saying to yourself, "Yeah, I want to do
whatever Jesus says, but how can I know what He wants me
to do? If I just knew...I would do it!"

You can know. God has given us three wonderful gifts in
this "following Christ" journey: His Word, the Holy Spirit,
and other believers.

1. His Word. The psalmist declares, "Your word is a lamp to my feet and a light to my path" (Ps. 119:105 ESV). The Bible will clearly guide you as you "resolve" to do all that Jesus asks. Even Jesus, when faced with temptation, responded with "It is written...." Soak up the Word. The more you know the Word of God, the more you will know God. As God's Word takes root in your heart and soul, resolve to follow its guidance—and whatever He says to you, do it.

2. Holy Spirit. Jesus gave us the Holy Spirit—our Helper—and promised that "he will teach you all things and bring to your remembrance all that I have said to you" (John 14:26 ESV). In John 16:13 Jesus added, "He [Holy Spirit] will guide you into all the truth." Listen and hear what Jesus says to do through the whispers of His Spirit.

3. Other Believers. The great apostle Paul reminded the Philippians, "What you have learned and received and heard and seen in me—practice these things..." (Phil. 4:9 ESV). Again in First Corinthians 11:1 (ESV) Paul admonishes, "Be imitators of me, as I am of Christ."

You *are* who you spend time with.

Each one of us needs spiritual leaders and "coaches" in our lives from whom we hear and see and learn and receive guidance in doing what Jesus says. Resolve to get more godly people speaking into your life. Make a resolution to soak in His Word…meditate and listen to His Holy Spirit…commune and fellowship with other Christians. And whatever Jesus says to you—*do it!*

I agree with Randy Alcorn who wrote:

> We fail to hear God's voice (in Scripture and through others and through the direct impressions put upon us by His Holy Spirit) and see His hand of providence in dozens of things that come our way throughout the day, and thousands throughout our lives…So we need to become more alert to seeking and hearing God's voice.[2]

PRAYER TO IGNITE

God, I want to follow You and finish strong in my journey. Fill me with Your Word and let my ears hear You when You say, "This is the way, walk in it."

ENDNOTES

1. Henry T. Blackaby, Claude B. King, *Experiencing God*, 33.
2. Randy Alcorn, "Is it possible to really hear God speak?" Eternal Perspective Ministries; www.epm.org/resources/2010/Mar/29/it-possible-really-hear-god-speak/; accessed 4/20/12.

REAL MEN, REAL LOVE

*Because he holds fast to me in love, I will
deliver him; I will protect him, because he
knows my name* (Psalm 91:14 ESV).

*God proved His love on the Cross. When Christ
hung, and bled, and died, it was God saying to
the world, "I love you."* —BILLY GRAHAM

What defines you? What one word encapsulates all of the
plans you have for your life?

For some it's *achievements*. For others it might be
possessions...prestige...power.

God has a different perspective. What matters to Him
most of all is love. In fact Jesus declared, *"By this all people
will know that you are my disciples, if you have love for one
another"* (John 13:35 ESV).

The word "love" is used in the English Standard Version
of the Bible more than 500 times. One of my favorites is found
in Psalm 91, which is often referred to as the "Psalm of Protection." In this psalm, beautiful metaphors—shelter, shadow,

fortress, refuge, shield, buckler, habitation, dwelling—are used to describe God's awesome power and protection.

In verse 14 God tells us what's behind His preservation and deliverance: *"Because he holds fast to me in love, I will deliver him. I will protect him, because he knows my name"* (Ps. 91:14 ESV).

In the original Hebrew, the term "holds fast" implies *binding* or *adhering* or *clinging*. When trouble, trials, and temptations rise up to meet us, the core of what God declares as necessary for us to experience His safeguard and protection is to *cling to Him in love*.

This image is echoed by Jesus when answering the question, "What is the greatest commandment?" *"He* [Jesus] *said to him, 'You shall love the Lord your God with all your heart and with all your soul and with all your mind'"* (Matt. 22:37 ESV).

We have no ability in ourselves to love God. We have the capacity to love Him with our entire being for only one reason—because He first loved us. *"In this is love, not that we have loved God, but that he loved us..."* (1 John 4:10 ESV).

When life's not the way it's supposed to be, when the wheels are coming off the bus, when nothing makes sense— *cling* to the Lord and rest assured of His "steadfast love" for you. He loved you so much that He stretched out His hands and let them drive nails into them. Jesus' kind of love is not for wimps, but for real men.

I also love the precept found in Romans 8 when the apostle Paul asks this critical question: *"Who shall separate us from the love of Christ? Shall tribulation, or distress, or*

persecution, or famine, or nakedness, or danger, or sword?"
(Rom. 8:35 ESV). Paul answers his own question in two parts.
He first declares that we are *"more than conquerors through
him who loved us"* (Rom. 8:37 ESV). The very things that
would seem to overwhelm us—trials, stress, money, danger—are actually opportunities for us to become conquerors,
warriors full of His power and strength. For example, the
waves that distress an ordinary swimmer produce great joy
to a surfer trained to ride and conquer them.

Paul then declares that *"neither death nor life, nor angels
nor rulers, nor things present nor things to come, nor powers,
nor height nor depth, nor anything else in all creation, will be
able to separate us from the love of God in Christ Jesus our
Lord"* (Rom. 8:38-39 ESV).

The remarkable truth is that nothing can wedge itself
between the undeserved, fathomless love of God and those
who call Him Father. Nothing.

Love is not for wimps. It takes a true man to love, a champion. Jesus showed His love for us by taking our place on the
cross, by letting those Roman soldiers drive nails into His
hands and feet. No, love is certainly not for wimps.

Stand strong, hold fast to Him and love Him with your
entire being.

PRAYER TO IGNITE

*God, I hold fast to You. Thank You for loving me
first. Thank You that nothing can separate us from
Your love. Teach me to love like You love.*

MADE FOR SOMETHING MORE

But those who wait on the Lord shall renew their strength; they shall mount up with wings like eagles... (Isaiah 40:31).

So the eagle lived and died a chicken, for that's what he thought he was. —ANTHONY DE MELLO

A chicken "ain't no" eagle.

Chickens are always looking down, cackling, while pecking around on the ground eating whatever they can find. It always amazed me that chickens can cackle and stuff their beaks at the same time! When they're out of chicken feed, they move on to dirt and bugs. They'll even eat their own— well, you get the picture.

Eagles on the other hand are always looking up to the sky longing for the high places. They live in tree tops and on mountain peaks and cruise at altitudes above the clouds. A bald eagle can soar to a height of 10,000 feet! Most chickens can fly four to six feet. When flying in storms, instead of letting the fierce winds hold them down, eagles spread their wings and use the wind to push them higher, breaking through the clouds to the calm sky above. Eagles fly above the storm, chickens run for cover!

Eagles were not created to live in chicken coops. Neither were you. God didn't say, "Those who wait upon the Lord shall mount up with wings like chickens!" Nope, He said, *"But those who wait on the Lord shall renew their strength; they shall mount up with wings like eagles…"* (Isa. 40:31). According to God, you were made for greater things than pecking around. You were made to soar. Who are you going to listen to—God or the chickens in your life? You may have people telling you to stop looking up, stop trying to get out of the coop, and just try to fit in with the crowd. But God's called you to more. You have a choice. You don't have to be intimidated by the chickens. You can fight the status quo; those who demand you compromise and try to hold you down!

If you listen to the chickens, I promise that you *will* stay grounded. Many well-intentioned people around you will try their level best to keep you in the coop. "What makes you think you're an eagle?" they'll ask. "You're just a chicken like the rest of us. Now start pecking!"

Jesus understood this mentality all too well. Read what they had to say about Him in Mark 6:1-6:

> *Then He went out from there and came to His own country…And…He began to teach in the synagogue. And many hearing Him were astonished, saying, "Where did this Man get these*

things? And what wisdom is this which is given to Him, that such mighty works are performed by His hands! Is this not the carpenter, the Son of Mary, and brother of James, Joses, Judas, and Simon? And are not His sisters here with us?" So they were offended at Him. But Jesus said to them, "A prophet is not without honor except in his own country, among his own relatives, and in his own house." Now He could do no mighty work there... because of their unbelief....

Did you get that? Instead of embracing Jesus and His obvious wisdom and the wonderful signs that followed Him, they were offended. "What gives you the right to do great and profound things?" they asked. "You're just one of us. Now start pecking!" Jesus could do incredible miracles everywhere except in His own hometown because of their chicken mentality.

Don't let the doubting voices of the chickens convince you that you're not an eagle. Don't let them keep you in the coop. Don't let your own doubt and fear keep you in the coop either. You're not a chicken. Spread your wings and soar!

PRAYER TO IGNITE

Lord, let me walk in truth listening to Your voice and acting on it. Help me to stand up to the chickens in my life who are trying to keep me down with their unbelief. Renew my strength and help me spread my wings and soar like an eagle.

Day 20

THE COURAGE TO FEAR

*Do not fear those who kill the body, but
are unable to kill the soul, but rather fear
Him who is able to destroy both soul and
body in hell* (Matthew 10:28 NASB).

*To fear the Lord is to be overwhelmed with
wonder before the greatness of God and his love.
It means that, because of his bright holiness
and magnificent love, you find him "fearfully
beautiful." That is why the more we experience
God's grace and forgiveness, the more we experience
a trembling awe and wonder before the greatness
of all that he is and has done for us. Fearing him
means bowing before him out of amazement at
his glory and beauty.* —TIMOTHY KELLER[1]

Teenage boy.

In a tree stand.

Late evening.

Bow hunting for whitetail deer.

What steps out of the edge of the woods?

A monster black bear. Six hundred, maybe seven hundred pounds.

It just hung around like it knew I was up there. Then just as the sun dipped below the tree line, it wandered back into the woods. It was my chance to get down and out of there! But how far in the woods did it go? Oh, did I mention that black bears can run up to 30 mph? When I came down out of the tree, do you think I had some fear in me? I walked on water all the way home!

There's a big difference between fearing God and being afraid. After receiving the Ten Commandments from God, Moses came down from the mountain and appeared before the Israelites. Witnessing thunder, lightning, and the manifest presence of God caused them to tremble with fear that God would destroy them. *"Moses said to the people, 'Do not be afraid. God has come to test you, so that the fear of God will be with you to keep you from sinning'"* (Exod. 20:20 NIV). Don't be afraid, but fear God? Sounds like a contradiction, but it's not. God doesn't want us to be afraid of Him; He invites us to approach Him, yet at the same time He wants us to be obedient to Him, respect Him, and avoid the consequences of sin.

"There is a fear that is slavish," writes John Piper, "that drives us away from God, and there is a fear that is sweet and draws us to God…God means for His power and holiness to kindle fear in us, not to drive us from Him, but to drive us to Him. His anger is against those who forsake Him and love other things more."[2]

Actually, proper fear of God leads us to courage. As men who fear God, we are not to fear other men—what they may say or think about us. When our focus is on God and on doing His will, our fear of God (that drives us to Him) over-shadows our fear of man. Then we are free to serve God all out, regardless of the outcome. *"Do not fear those who kill the body, but are unable to kill the soul,"* Jesus taught, *"but rather fear Him who is able to destroy both soul and body in hell"* (Matt. 10:28 NASB). Our fear of God should produce boldness in the face of men who would oppose us.

In our hearts, we know we ought to fear God, but our fleshy nature battles against us in an attempt to keep us from doing so. In the same way, as men we know instinc-tively that we ought to be courageous, but again, we are caught in the conflict between flesh and spirit—between what we know we ought to do and what we often choose to do. Instead of acting with courage, men today too often choose not to act at all.

In the face of danger, in the face of adversity, a man is to respond with courage. To stand up and do the right thing at the right time. If a husband is going to fulfill his calling to love and lead his wife, he is going to need to draw on his courage and convictions. He will have to stay alert to spiri-tual and physical danger. He will have to stand firm in the faith and to lovingly lead his wife to stand firm with him. He will have to be courageous and act like a man.

It takes courage to stand in the face of an ungodly cul-ture where, *"evil men and seducers [are waxing] worse and worse"* (2 Tim. 3:13) and say "No" to *"the lust of the flesh, and the lust of the eyes and the boastful pride of life"* (1 John 2:16 NASB).

Let me fear only those things that drive me to boldness in God.

PRAYER TO IGNITE

God, Your Word says the fear of God is the beginning of wisdom. I ask that You empower me to be confident and courageous and stand for You.

ENDNOTES

1.   http://kellerquotes.com/the-fear-of-the-lord/; accessed 6/4/14.

2.   John Piper, *The Purifying Power of Living by Faith in Future Grace* (New York: Multnomah Books, 1995), 242-244.

YOUR OPPONENT

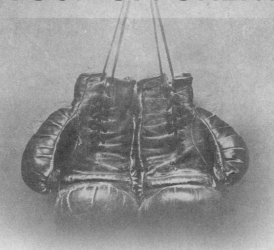

In boxing, you have to be skilled enough and have trained hard enough to know how many different ways you can counterattack in any situation, at any moment. —Jimmy Smits

In boxing you create a strategy to beat each new opponent, it's just like chess. —Lennox Lewis

Be sober, be vigilant; because your adversary the devil walks about like a roaring lion, seeking whom he may devour (1 Peter 5:8).

Simon, Simon, Satan has asked to sift all of you as wheat (Luke 22:31 NIV).

PRAYING ALWAYS

Pray without ceasing, give thanks in all circumstances; for this is the will of God in Christ Jesus for you (1 Thessalonians 5:17-18 ESV).

The greatest deterrent to an effective prayer life is the belief that everything has to be right before I can pray. —RICHARD FOSTER

I've heard a few prayers during my lifetime that seemed to go on forever. You? Ugh. But others, every word seemed so right. Time stood still. Prayers you could feel, that lingered after the last Amen. My dad prayed like that. I could hear them over and over again. More than words, they were prayers that entered the presence of God.

Raw.

Real.

Honest.

That's the key to powerful prayer.

God just wants you to come as you are. Martin Luther said, "The fewer words, the better the prayer." It's spirit.

It's heart. It's thought. Sometimes no matter what position your body is in, your soul is on its knees. *That is unceasing prayer.* God loves it. You know why? Because He's on your mind and that's the first step to getting your heart right—and by the way, living in His will.

"*Rejoice always, pray without ceasing, in everything give thanks; this is the will of God in Christ Jesus for you*" (1 Thess. 5:16-18). Think that way. Pray that way.

When you pray do you ever feel like your words are bouncing off the ceiling, not going anywhere? Like your voice is the only one you can hear and the heavens are silent? If you've felt this way, take heart. Apostle Paul said, "*praying always with all prayer and supplication in the Spirit, being watchful to this end with all perseverance and supplication for all the saints*" (Eph. 6:18). Jesus said "*...that men always ought to pray and not lose heart*" (Luke 18:1). The implication of that statement is that some prayers are going to require perseverance. Mark Batterson wrote:

> Bold prayers honor God, and God honors bold prayers. God isn't offended by your biggest dreams or boldest prayers. He is offended by anything less. If your prayers aren't impossible to you, they are insulting to God.... Most of us don't get what we want because we quit praying. We give up too easily. We give up too soon.[1]

Be steadfast in your prayers; walk in step with the Spirit and learn His voice as He speaks to you. Remember, James 5:16 says, "*...The effective, fervent prayer of a righteous man* *avails much."* Your prayers make a difference. They are affecting outcomes. Virtually all the giants of the faith—the Moodys and Wesleys and the like, had one thing in common. They were men of persevering prayer.

PRAYER TO IGNITE

Holy Spirit, prepare my heart and mind to hear You speak. Help me to pray always and not lose heart.

ENDNOTE

1. Mark Batterson, *The Circle Maker: Praying Circles Around Your Biggest Dreams and Greatest Fears* (Grand Rapids, MI: Zondervan, 2011).

Day 22

BEFORE THE FALL

For those who exalt themselves will be humbled, and those who humble themselves will be exalted (Matthew 23:12 NIV).

...that beating taught me humility in this sense. It taught me never to think that I was better than anyone else. It taught me that on any given day, you can be beaten. This always helped push me to prepare for my bouts. A few years later, after I knocked out Joe Frazier and won the heavyweight title, I forgot that lesson in humility and again, I had to pay the price by getting beaten and embarrassed by Muhammad Ali in Zaire. —GEORGE FOREMAN

When growing up, remember the punk with the chip on his shoulder, the cocky kid you wanted to jack? Something inside us loathes arrogance in others. We naturally resist it. And just in case you need to be reminded, when it comes to personal pride, there's always someone bigger and better. We've all heard the old saying, "Pride goes before a fall." It's actually biblical. Proverbs 16:18 says, *"Pride goes before destruction, and a haughty spirit before a fall."*

Humility is a subject that great thinkers of the world take seriously. John Buchan, British diplomat and author, declared, "Without humility there can be no humanity." Solomon said, *"A man's pride will bring him low, but the humble in spirit will retain honor"* (Prov. 29:23) and *"When pride comes, then comes shame; but with the humble is wisdom"* (Prov. 11:2). Pride brings shame; humility brings wisdom. Jesus put it this way, *"whoever exalts himself will be humbled, and he who humbles himself will be exalted"* (Matt. 23:12). Sounds to me like humility is a pretty serious subject. But what is authentic humility?

FOUR QUICK POINTS OF AUTHENTIC HUMILITY

I. Humble people recognize their dependency on God.

Dependency on God does not mean we shouldn't use our heads. Dependency is looking to God for direction and recognizing His ability to orchestrate the affairs of our lives—acknowledging God's role by seeking Him for direction instead of forging out on our own presumptuously. *"In all your ways acknowledge Him, and He shall direct your paths"* (Prov. 3:6).

2. Humble people are secure in who they are.

Humble people do not belittle themselves. They do not act insignificantly or inadequately because they know they are valuable just as they are, flaws and all. Therefore, there is no need to prove anything or elevate themselves. They know who they are in Christ, that they are valuable because *"God so loved the world that he gave his one and only Son, that whoever believes in him shall not perish but have eternal life"* (John 3:16 NIV). They know that there is nothing they can do that will make Him love them less and there is nothing they can do that will make Him love them more.

3. Humble people are interdependent.

They are aware that they do not know all the answers and that there may be others who are more intelligent, have more experience, and are more gifted. They are not independent or codependent; they are interdependent. They are team players who perceive the value of input from others. It's staggering what we can accomplish if we are humble enough to surround ourselves with the right people.

4. Humble people are real.

Keith Miller wrote in his book *A Hunger for Healing* that "Humility is seeing ourselves as we actually are, good and bad, strong and weak, and acting authentically on those truths." Humble people have looked in the mirror of their souls and have taken an honest inventory. They realize there will always be the need for growth and that conforming into Christ's image is a lifelong process. Humble people understand their need for grace in their own lives and therefore can give grace to others. Apostle Paul was a great example. He knew he was a new creation in Christ, covered in His righteousness. But the same Paul who taught us that also said, *"I am less than the least of all the Lord's people"* (Eph. 3:8 NIV). Paul understood true humility. Do you?

PRAYER TO IGNITE

Lord, Your Word says there is wisdom in humility. Teach me authentic humility—to depend on You and to know that even though I have faults, because of what Christ did for me, I am valuable. Help me to rest in Your security.

Day 23

A LOW WHISPER

And after the earthquake a fire, but the Lord
was not in the fire. And after the fire the sound
of a low whisper (1 Kings 19:12 ESV).

God will speak to the hearts of those who
prepare themselves to hear.... —A.W. TOZER[1]

Highs and lows.

One minute we experience a victorious spiritual break-
through and are on top of the world.

The next minute the raw realities of life assault the very
core of our faith in everyday life.

As if that isn't enough, the enemy loves to then whisper
in our ears, *"What a loser," "You really can't do anything*
right, can you?" "God isn't listening," "You will never be
used," "You'd better run for your life," "God isn't really there
for you..."

And too often we believe him.

Elijah understood this. Under the rule of King Ahab and
his wicked wife, Jezebel, the children of Israel had turned

their back on God and worshipped Baal. In a bold attempt to turn the people's hearts back to God, Elijah calls the prophets of Baal to a contest. A sacrifice was prepared and Elijah challenges, *"And you call upon the name of your god, and I will call upon the name of the Lord, and the God who answers by fire, he is God"* (1 Kings 18:24 ESV).

The deceived prophets cried out to Baal all day and no fire fell. Elijah then takes his turn. He prays to the *"God of Abraham, Isaac, and Israel...then the fire of the Lord fell and consumed the burnt offering...and when all of the people saw it, they fell on their faces and said, 'The Lord, he is God; the Lord, he is God.'"* (1 Kings 18:36-39 ESV).

Elijah experiences a stunning victory.

A short six verses later, Jezebel threatens to kill Elijah *"by this time tomorrow"* (1 Kings 19:2 ESV). Then *"he was afraid, and he arose and ran for his life"* (1 Kings 19:3 ESV). Elijah sits down under a tree and asks to die – *"O Lord, take away my life..."* (1 Kings 19:4 ESV) and then falls asleep.

His triumph turned to discouragement, discouragement to depression, and depression to despair. What a turn of events.

But just when we think God isn't there—that He's abandoned us, that the whole world would be better off without us—God is ready to meet us at each point of need.

Consider what happens next. An angel of the Lord wakes up Elijah and gives him this simple instruction, *"Arise and eat."* Elijah looked and there was *"a cake baked on hot stones and a jar of water."* And he *"arose and ate and drank, and went in the strength of that food forty days and forty nights to Horeb, the mount of God"* (1 Kings 19:5-8 ESV).

If you're in a pit, it just might be that you need real food and sleep.

Then notice verse 12. God lovingly reaches out to His servant. He doesn't leave him hopeless. He speaks in the *"sound of a low whisper"* reassuring him of His presence, power, and provision: *"And after the earthquake a fire, but the Lord was not in the fire. And after the fire the sound of a low whisper."*

Author Richard Exley wrote:

> God began the restoration process by giving Elijah a spiritual experience based on intimacy rather than power, a gentle whisper rather than a roaring wind. Why? Because power is seldom what we need when we have come to the end of ourselves. At those times, we need relationship—a gentle whisper assuring us of our value.[2]

God knows your name. He is all powerful but also intensely personal. He is speaking to you. Chances are it's just beneath the clutter and commotion, a low whisper. In times of despair we must slow the process and lean into His voice—listening and obeying as He conforms our will to His.

PRAYER TO IGNITE

Lord, prepare my ears to hear Your gentle whispers that cut through the despair in my life, bringing reassurance of my value and Your presence.

ENDNOTES

1.   A.W. Tozer, *The Root of Righteousness: Tapping the Bedrock to True Spirituality* (Camp Hill, PA: Christian Publications, 1986), 21.

2.   Richard Exley, *Man of Valor, Every Man's Quest for a Life of Honor, Conviction, and Character* (Lakeland, FL: White Stone Books, Inc., 2005), 17.

Day 24

A MIGHTY WHAT?

*So he [Gideon] said to Him, "O my Lord,
how can I save Israel? Indeed my clan is the
weakest in Manasseh, and I am the least
in my father's house" (Judges 6:15).*

*You may feel it is too late, that you've been
robbed of your destiny. Don't give up! God has
a plan for your life even if you can't see it. As
a man created in His image, you are destined
for greatness. Whether you realize it or not you
were created to be a valiant man! No matter
how foreign that may seem to you, it's true. You
were created to conquer!* —RICHARD EXLEY[1]

Get this picture. An Angel of the Lord appears before Gideon
and announces, *"The Lord is with you, you mighty man of
valor!"* (Judg. 6:12). But wait! A man of valor? Really? The
Bible says that when the angel appeared, Gideon was threshing wheat down in a winepress.

*The angel of the Lord came and sat down under
the oak in Ophrah that belonged to Joash the*

Abiezrite, where his son Gideon was threshing wheat in a winepress to keep it from the Midianites (Judges 6:11 NIV).

At first glance no big deal, but threshing wheat in a winepress was strange indeed. Wheat and tares (weeds) grew up together and had to be separated. This process normally occurred in specially made threshing floors out in open fields where there was wind. The wheat and tares had to be thrown into the air so the wind could blow away the tares letting the heavier wheat fall to the ground. Winepresses, on the other hand, were located down in pits carved out of rock.

Now let me ask you this: How do you thresh wheat if you're in a pit? Not very well. There's no wind!

Again, I have to ask, why was this so-called *man of valor* threshing wheat down in a winepress? Here's why; the Midianites, one of Israel's arch enemies, had been oppressing them, doing some pretty nasty stuff. One of the things they did was to swoop down from the hillside, where they'd been spying from, and steal the wheat as soon as it had been threshed. Gideon was threshing in the winepress because he was hiding from the enemy. All of Israel was afraid and hiding out.

Suddenly this Angel appears to him and says, *"The Lord is with you, you mighty man of valor!"* Gideon, of course, is convinced the angel's heavenly GPS sent him to the wrong address. At which point, the two of them have a little discussion. Gideon informs the Angel of all the horrible things the Midianites had been doing to God's people. Gideon asked,

If we are God's people and He's with us, *"why then has all this happened to us?"* (Judg. 6:13). Sounds familiar, doesn't it? When bad stuff happens, we so often assume that God is not with us.

Unfazed by Gideon's argument, the Angel responds by giving the mighty man of valor a bold assignment, *"Go in this might of yours, and you shall save Israel from the hand of the Midianites"* (Judg. 6:14).

I can see Gideon choking on a kernel of wheat. *"Me? Yeah right. What might? Didn't you hear what just I said?"* Then Gideon tries to talk some more sense into the Angel. *"How can I save Israel? Indeed my clan is the weakest in Manasseh, and I am the least in my father's house"* (Judg. 6:15). In other words, "Don't you get it? I come from a long line of losers. You've got the wrong man! I'm not the guy."

The Angel doesn't even blink an eye, just continues. *"Surely I will be with you, and you shall defeat the Midianites as one man"* (Judg. 6:16).

As the rest of the story goes, because of his unbelief, Gideon throws out a series of fleeces to convince himself that what God is saying is true. In the end, Gideon does obey, albeit skeptically, and God uses him to deliver Israel—His family.

Gideon measured himself by his past. He saw himself as *the least of the weakest clan*. God, however, measured Gideon according to what he could be—based on his true identity—a mighty man of valor who would obey and deliver Israel.

How about you? Are you hiding in a winepress trying to thresh wheat? Are you afraid? Paralyzed by a fear of failure? Of rejection? Of the past? Of never being used? Do you see yourself as God sees you? If you've trusted in Christ, then He is in you and here's what God says about you:

> *His divine power has given to us all things that pertain to life and godliness...* (2 Peter 1:3).

> *I have been crucified with Christ; it is no longer I who live, but Christ lives in me* (Galatians 2:20).

> *Now thanks be to God who always leads us in triumph in Christ, and through us diffuses the fragrance of His knowledge in every place* (2 Corinthians 2:14).

> *For God has not given us a spirit of fear, but of power and of love and of a sound mind* (2 Timothy 1:7).

> *Though an army besiege me, my heart will not fear; though war break out against me, even then will I be confident. For in the day of trouble God will keep me safe in his dwelling...* (Psalm 27:3,5 NIV).

Regardless of how you *feel* about yourself, trust in what God says about you and get back in the fight!

PRAYER TO IGNITE

Lord, give me the eyes to see myself as You do. Empower me to act according to what You say about me and with the knowledge that I am more than a conqueror through You. Without You I am nothing, but with You I can do all things.

ENDNOTE

1. Richard Exley, *Man of Valor, Every Man's Quest for a Life of Honor, Conviction, and Character,* 7.

GET UP AND GET MOVING!

Through laziness, the rafters sag; because of idle hands, the house leaks (Ecclesiastes 10:18 NIV).

Procrastination is one of the most common and deadliest of diseases and its toll on success and happiness is heavy. —WAYNE GRETZKY

It's been said in different ways by different people. "You have to do today what others are not doing, so you can do tomorrow what others can't do." My mother put it this way, "How long you gonna sleep in that bed? Get up and get moving!"

You know, procrastination is like a credit card. It's a lot of fun until you get the bill. It also may be one of the enemy's most effective tools in his assault on God's children. So often we put off today what can be done tomorrow. The enemy uses schemes and tactics to ensnare us and distract us from doing God's will for our lives. He can use good things to distract us from even better things. We can't afford to lose our focus or spend time on those things that don't really matter.

If the enemy can keep us struggling with things from our past we can keep putting off doing what he's called us to do. You were designed for a specific purpose. Pastor Rick Warren and author of the mega-bestseller *The Purpose Driven Life* gives five biblical reasons we procrastinate: indecision, perfectionism, fear, anger, and laziness. Let's take a closer look at these five from Rick Warren's blog.

1.   **Indecision.** "A double minded man is unstable in all he does." (James 1:8 LB). ...Indecision causes you to postpone buying a car, choosing a college, getting married, buying new clothes, changing a job.

2.   **Perfectionism.** "If you wait for perfect conditions, you'll never get anything done!" (Ecclesiastes 11:4 LB) If you wait for things to be perfect, you're going to wait a long time. 3. **Fear.** "The fear of man is a trap." (Proverbs 29:25 LB) Have you been postponing going to the dentist? Or having that needed surgery? Or getting into marriage counseling? Sharing your faith at work? Ask yourself, "What am I afraid of?"

4.   **Anger.** "A lazy person is as bad as someone who is destructive" (Prov. 18:9 GNT). ...Procrastination is passive resistance. I don't want to do it because I don't like you telling me to do what I have to do. Anger causes us to put things off.

5. **Laziness.** "Lazy people want much but get little, while the diligent are prospering." (Proverbs 13:4 LB) One of the most popular words in America is "easy." If it's easy, we like it. If it's hard, we don't like it. Can you imagine a best seller titled, Ten Difficult Steps to Change Your Life or Fifteen Difficult Ways to Get in Shape? If it's easy, we like it. If it's hard, we don't like it.[1]

Stop putting things off. Get out of your comfort zone. Do what you've been dreading and get it out of the way. Do it now! If you don't know where to start, do the next right thing.

Hebrews 10:24 says to stir up love and good works. Good works don't just occur. They have to be stirred up. Let God's Spirit stir you up to do what He's called you to do. Stop procrastinating and start obeying God. How long you gonna stay in that bed? Get up and get moving!

PRAYER TO IGNITE

God, empower me to do the work You have called me to do. Help me to not delay but to be stirred up to good works.

ENDNOTE

1. Rick Warren, Daily Hope, "Why Do I Procrastinate?" August 18, 2010; purposedriven.com/blogs/dailyhope/index.html; accessed 6/4/14.

SLIGHTLY BENT

...run with endurance the race that is set before us, looking to Jesus... (Hebrews 12:1-2 ESV).

I'm seeing a lot of the problems right now. We've got players hurt from time to time, we had a very tough loss in New York, and it kind of gets you to say, "What?" Man, I'm looking around at the circumstances and I'm saying "Hey, I can't control all this." ...I'm at a point right now where I really have to say to the Lord, "Hey look, I'm gonna try to not look at my circumstances. We're 2-3 right now, we've had three tough losses. I don't want to look at those circumstances, Lord, I just want to look at you and I want to stay focused on you and I want to say to you, 'save me.'" —COACH JOE GIBBS of the Washington Redskins, before the Titans game

You look at it a lot, but do you see things clearly? Check out the mirror on your car's passenger side. Do you notice anything? There's a little message across the bottom that reads, *"Objects in mirror are closer than they appear."* That's because the mirror is slightly bent to give a wider field of vision. But the images are distorted. Things seem farther away than they actually are. Not realizing this could be dangerous. Even disastrous. You must pay close attention when looking into *this* kind of this mirror.

You know, we live in a world that's kind of bent like those mirrors. We see reflections from the culture and society around us, but it's critical to realize that things are not always as they seem. Satan is the prince of the power of the air and he is referred to as an *angel of light*. Some of what you see of this world may look enticing, even right and spiritual, but partaking of them will end in confusion and heartache. Proverbs 16:25 says, *"There is a way that seems right to a man, But its end is the way of death."*

The apostle Paul reminds us, *"For now we see in a mirror dimly"* (1 Cor. 13:12 ESV). The Greek word for "dimly" is *ainigma* and paints a picture of a vague, murky riddle. Life's reflection can be unclear some days—a puzzle that seems obscure and even unrecognizable. Perhaps this is why the writer of Hebrews admonishes us to *"run with endurance the race that is set before us, looking to Jesus..."* (Heb. 12:1-2 ESV). When we fix our gaze on Jesus and see His reflection, the distortion of the pace, pain, and pressure of life becomes refocused and redirected. Feelings no longer take control and become our reality.

When we are focused on Christ, an amazing thing happens. His image is reflected onto us. Over time, we become more and more transformed into His image. Romans 12:2 says, *"And do not be conformed to this world, but be transformed by the renewing of your mind."* Then as we are transformed into His image, the life of Christ can be reflected from us into the lives of those around us. That's how it works. People need to see the reflection of Christ in us. When they do, it can cause them to hunger and thirst for God. Your life can be a powerful instrument in the Holy Spirit's hand to draw others to Christ.

Is life unclear? Confusing? Ask God to help you see with eyes for Him. And He promises that one day all will be *perfectly clear* when we see Him face-to-face. Alan Redpath explains it this way:

> The man who gazes upon and contemplates day by day the face of the Lord Jesus Christ, and who has caught the glow of the reality that the Lord is not a theory but an indwelling power and force in his life, is as a mirror reflecting the glory of the Lord.

As you go through your daily life, fix your gaze upon Him and be transformed.

PRAYER TO IGNITE

Jesus, I need You. Empower me to take my eyes off of myself and the world around me and fix my vision on You. As I do, I will become a reflection of You to those around me who need You.

Day 27

IS HE OR ISN'T HE?

*If only for this life we have hope in
Christ, we are of all people most to be
pitied* (1 Corinthians 15:19 NIV).

*What changed these very ordinary men (who were
such cowards that they did not dare stand too near
the cross in case they got involved) into heroes who
would stop at nothing? A swindle? Hallucination?
Spooky nonsense in a darkened room? Or Somebody
quietly doing what he said he'd do—walk right
through death?* —J.B. PHILLIPS, *Is God at Home?*

On January 9, 1966, *The New York Times* proclaimed in giant letters, "God Is Dead...!" A few months later on April 8 spread across the front cover of *Time Magazine* was the question "Is God Dead?" More recently, the movie "God's Not Dead" had a record-breaking debut at the theatres.

The question is simple.

Is He or isn't He?

We ask ourselves that question every day.

Let's get real here. Either God *is* alive, Jesus *did* in fact rise from the dead, and heaven *is* our eternal home—or we're all just a bunch of fools chasing some fantasy to soothe our consciences and comfort our souls. If God is not real and Jesus did not rise, we should all just eat, drink, and be merry, because we're wasting our time!

Apostle Paul had an opinion about the subject and he made some pretty bold statements concerning it:

> *If Christ was not raised from the dead, then what we preach to you is worth nothing. Your faith in Christ is worth nothing. That makes us all liars because we said that God raised Christ from the dead...If Christ was not raised from the dead, your faith is worth nothing and you are still living in your sins"* (1 Corinthians 15:14-15,17 New Life Version).

Paul continued, *"If only for this life we have hope in Christ, we are of all people most to be pitied"* (1 Cor. 15:19 NIV). Paul knew that Christ was raised. He saw Him and spent a significant part of his ministry telling people what he saw. Before King Agrippa in Rome, Paul said:

> *While...I journeyed to Damascus with authority and commission from the chief priests, at midday, O king, along the road I saw a light from heaven, brighter than the sun, shining around me and those who journeyed with me. And when we all had fallen to the ground, I heard a voice speaking to me and saying in the Hebrew language, "Saul,*

Saul, why are you persecuting Me? It is hard for
you to kick against the goads." So I said, "Who
are You, Lord?" And He said, "I am Jesus, whom
you are persecuting. But rise and stand on your
feet; for I have appeared to you for this purpose,
to make you a minister and a witness both of the
things which you have seen and of the things which
I will yet reveal to you" (Acts 26:12-16).

When Paul wrote these words, in essence he was saying,
"Hey, guys, if we came to Christ to have a grand ole time
in this life, then we are all a bunch of idiots, because the
moment we became Christ-followers our lives really started
to get messy." Paul knew what he was talking about. Before
he met Christ on the Damascus Road he had it all—wealth,
position, prestige. Afterward, not so much. Listen to his
own words.

...I have worked much harder, been in prison more
frequently, been flogged more severely, and been
exposed to death again and again. Five times I
received from the Jews the forty lashes minus one.
Three times I was beaten with rods, once I was
pelted with stones, three times I was shipwrecked,
I spent a night and a day in the open sea, I have
been constantly on the move. I have been in danger
from rivers, in danger from bandits, in danger
from my fellow Jews, in danger from Gentiles; in
danger in the city, in danger in the country, in
danger at sea; and in danger from false believers.

I have labored and toiled and have often gone without sleep; I have known hunger and thirst and have often gone without food; I have been cold and naked" (2 Corinthians 11:23-27 NIV).

Oh, did I forget? Every one of the apostles, except John who was exiled, were eventually martyred. During the rule of Emperor Nero in the first century, thousands upon thousands of Christians were tortured to death. The Roman historian Tacitus wrote that Christians:

died in torments, and their torments were embittered by insult and derision. Some were nailed on crosses; others sewn up in the skins of wild beasts and exposed to the fury of dogs; others, again, smeared over with combustible materials, were used as torches to illuminate the darkness of the night.[1]

Quick, sign me up!

Listen, we don't become Christians in order to gain a better standing in the community, to attain success in our careers, or even to fix our relationship problems. All of those are simply potential by-products of our faith. They may or may not happen. If our faith isn't real, then we have been greatly deceived and are to be pitied.

There is nothing wrong with working hard to experience the best this life has to offer. But we can never forget that our greatest reward will never come in this life, rather in the life to come. Our ultimate assurance is that we will one day overcome our final enemy, death. Paul says in First Corinthians 15:20 (NIV), *"But Christ has indeed been raised from the dead...."* Because he had experienced the risen Christ, Paul could write, *"our light affliction, which is but for a moment, is working for us a far more exceeding and eternal weight of glory"* (2 Cor. 4:17). All those hardships Paul described earlier he calls light afflictions when compared to eternal glory.

The good news: God *is* alive.

And because He is—it changes everything.

PRAYER TO IGNITE

Lord, I know in this life there are hardships, but I believe You are real and alive, and that one day I will live eternally with You.

ENDNOTE

1.   John Foxe, *Foxe's Annals of Martyrs* (Burlington, ON: Inspirational Promotions, 1960), 33.

THE MOST IMPORTANT THING

*Above all else, guard your heart, for everything
you do flows from it (Proverbs 4:23 NIV).*

*Satan uses all kinds of weapons to attack our heart.
For me, these attacks often come in the form of
some circumstance that leads to disappointment,
discouragement, or even disillusionment. In these
situations, I am tempted to quit—to walk off
the field and surrender.* —MICHAEL HYATT

The Hebrew word for "heart" in Proverbs 4:23 is *soul—the
seat of appetites, emotions, and passions—our core self.*
Whichever way you interpret it, we are to keep it *"Above
all else."* Why? Because how we choose to guard our hearts
against the vain philosophies, corruption, and hardness of
the world will determine the course of our lives, *"...every-
thing you do flows from it."* The Hebrew connotation for
the word "guard" in the opening passage refers to the act of
guarding someone closely as a Roman solider would guard a

prisoner. Often a Roman soldier was charged with his life. If the prisoner escaped, the soldier would be killed. We are to guard our hearts with that same intensity— diligently, attentively, aggressively.

The apostle Peter said it another way:

> ...*Make every effort to add to your faith goodness; and to goodness, knowledge; and to knowledge, self-control; and to self-control, perseverance; and to perseverance, godliness; and to godliness, mutual affection; and to mutual affection, love. For if you possess these qualities in increasing measure, they will keep you from being ineffective and unproductive in your knowledge of our Lord Jesus Christ. ...For if you do these things, you will never stumble.... So I will always remind you of these things, even though you know them and are firmly established in the truth you now have*" (2 Peter 1:5-8,10,12 NIV).

In other words, men, make every effort, make it an extreme priority to guard the truths of God's Word that are planted in your heart. Keep focused on the right things. The enemy wants to strip away our joy; to accuse us in times when we are struggling with life's trials. He would try to steal our faith in Christ in times of pain and suffering. This is when we have to rise up and guard our hearts. Remind ourselves to "*fight the good fight of faith, lay hold on eternal life...*" (1 Tim. 6:12). In times of difficulty we need to hold on to our hope in the living God. "*Let us hold fast the confession of our hope without wavering, for He who promised is faithful"* (Heb. 10:23).

The enemy wants to distract us from our destiny. He is very real and is seeking to destroy us. Keep your guard up. As Peter warns, we need to stick to the basics *"even though you know them and are firmly established in the truth."* If we do, we *"will never fall"* (2 Pet. 1:10 ESV).

PRAYER TO IGNITE

God, help me to be firmly grounded in Your truths. My hope is in You. I resist the enemy's attempts to distract or discourage me from following Your Word. Help me to guard my heart above all else.

TAKING PUNCHES BUT NOT GOING DOWN

We are hard-pressed on every side, yet not crushed; we are perplexed, but not in despair; persecuted, but not forsaken; struck down, but not destroyed (2 Corinthians 4:8-9).

God, I know that if you bring me to it, you will bring me through it. I know you have a plan, but quite honestly I don't see it right now. But I know it's there. I know I have to believe. I know I need to have faith. I have to trust you. And I do trust you. But it's hard right now. —DREW BREES[1]

One of my favorite *Rocky* movie scenes of all time is in film number III when Clubber Lang (Mr. T) is being interviewed about his upcoming fight with Rocky Balboa. After being asked what his prediction was, Mr. T, with his Mohawk haircut and enraged eyes, stares into the camera, and growls, "Pain." Later, in the ring, he followed up on his prediction by destroying Rocky, knocking him out.

It was brutal.

There are times when life delivers Mr. T kind of blows, and like Rocky we don't absorb them and get knocked out. For Rocky it looked like it was all over. That may be you. It looks like everything is over. But if you saw the movie, you know what happened next. Rocky reassessed his situation. Saw himself as the champion he knew he was. He then made a choice and reached down deep for inspiration. He retrained. He ignited and got back in the fight. This time the results were different. It was lights out for Mr. T.

It's a given. Men who are in Christ *will* face trials, hardships, and suffering at some point in their lives. God takes you through tough times of training and uses them to bring about His character. How we respond to them is a reflection of our trust in Him to produce perseverance, character, and hope in us.

On many occasions, the warrior David was hard pressed, perplexed, and struck down. He took jabs, punches from life and his enemies. Once, he cried out to God, "...*have mercy on me, for I am desolate and afflicted. The troubles of my heart have enlarged; bring me out of my distresses! Look on my affliction and my pain...*" (Ps. 25:16-18).

This is David the Giant killer. The same one who killed a bear and a lion and led Israel to victory! He's a warrior, a leader. Yet, he experienced great pain. What set David apart as *"a man after God's own heart"* however, was in the midst of his failures and pain he always knew he belonged to God. Once, when David and his men approached the city of Ziklag, they discovered that the Amalekites had raided it, burned it with fire, and carried off all the women and children. Ziklag was a city under David's domain. David was devastated as were his followers. What got him through, however, was the way he strengthened himself, not in people, not in getting encouragement from friends and yes-men, but in the Lord.

> *Now David was greatly distressed, for the people spoke of stoning him, because the soul of all the people was grieved, every man for his sons and his daughters. But David strengthened himself in the Lord his God* (1 Samuel 30:6).

Wow. David's only hope of encouragement was in the Lord his God.

David never denied the reality of his situation, but he knew the Lord was *his* God. Do you know that? Listen to what David says just one verse later after all his lamenting, *"Keep my soul, and deliver me; let me not be ashamed; for I put my trust in You"* (Ps. 25:20). David chose, by an act of his will, to put his trust in God. In the next chapter he wrote, *"I have trusted also in the Lord; therefore I shall not slide"* (Ps. 26:1 KJV).

"Therefore I shall not slide," I like that. Everything around David appeared to be crumbling and slipping away, yet David affirmed that regardless what it looked like, he was not going to be moved. Like a champion boxer, because of his confidence in God, his feet were firm and set, and he would not swerve away from his godly purpose of life. At the end of the chapter he declares, *"My foot stands in an even place; in the congregations I will bless the Lord"* (Ps. 26:12). In other words, "Whatever I'm going through, I have taken my stand. I'm firmly planted on solid ground.

I'm not moving, and I will proclaim God's goodness to those around me."

David acknowledges God and refuses to blame Him of injustice. He embraces the struggle and holds fast to his faith in the Almighty God. Like the apostle Paul, he understood with God in our corner, *"We are hard-pressed on every side, yet not crushed; we are perplexed, but not in despair; persecuted, but not forsaken; struck down, but not destroyed"* (2 Cor. 4:8-9).

Sometimes our biggest battle is to believe God is with us when trials assault us. It doesn't seem fair that bad things happen, when we are in pain or when we are watching the ones we love suffer. During these times there are no easy answers. We just have to keep fighting. Like David, we must set our feet firm, take courage, and choose to believe God is real and alive and working His purposes in us. Refuse to let the punches and jabs that life can throw cause you to lose heart. *"He gives power to the weak, and to those who have no might He increases strength"* (Isa. 40:29).

PRAYER TO IGNITE

God, Your word says as long as I'm in the world there will be tribulations. Help me to embrace the struggle. Show me how to have peace in the midst of my trials and strengthen myself in You, to know that You, Lord, are my God.

ENDNOTE

1.   Drew Brees, *Coming Back Stronger: Unleashing the Hidden Power of Adversity* (Carol Stream, IL: Tyndale House Publishers, Inc., 2011).

Day 30

REMEMBER THIS

*Evildoers and impostors will go from bad
to worse, deceiving and being deceived. But
as for you [Timothy], continue in what you
have learned... (2 Timothy 3:13-14 NIV).*

*You have enemies? Good. That means
you've stood up for something sometime
in your life.* —WINSTON CHURCHILL

Remember that special coach who cared about you, the one
who wanted to bring out your best potential? Remember him
grabbing your facemask and pulling your face so close to
his that you could feel his breath, maybe smell it? The coach
got your attention because he had something important to
say, to make a point he didn't want you to miss. Maybe he
slapped you upside the helmet. You got the point.

When the apostle Paul penned his second letter to Timothy, time was short. He could feel the executioner's breath
on his neck. Knowing this was his last correspondence with
his spiritual son, Paul chose his words carefully. These were
important words. He didn't want Timothy to miss it. In the

first couple of chapters, Paul encourages Timothy to, *"fear not, be strong in the grace that is in Jesus Christ, hold fast, endure hardness as a good soldier, study to show himself approved, shun profane and vain words, and flee youthful lusts."* But then, in chapter 3, Paul gives Timothy a prophetic warning.

> *But mark this: There will be terrible times in the last days. People will be lovers of themselves, lovers of money, boastful, proud, abusive, disobedient to their parents, ungrateful, unholy, without love, unforgiving, slanderous, without self-control, brutal, not lovers of the good, treacherous, rash, conceited, lovers of pleasure rather than lovers of God—having a form of godliness but denying its power. Have nothing to do with such people* (2 Timothy 3:1-5 NIV).

Sounds like the daily news! Paul understood fully the direction that society was headed and the battles Timothy would be facing. He knew there would be times when the whole world would be against him and he would be forced to stand alone, that he was going to have to fight for the things he knew were right.

What battles are you in? What has come against you? Where do you feel defeated?

Continuing his prophetic warning, Paul tells Timothy that, *"Evildoers and impostors will go from bad to worse, deceiving and being deceived. But as for you, continue in what you have learned..."* (2 Tim. 3:13-14 NIV).

By saying those words *"But as for you,"* Paul is letting Timothy know that regardless of the world's direction and pressures, he is set apart for a higher purpose. At times, this means standing alone against the tide of evil and making conscious choices to fight the fight of faith.

As men in today's culture we too have been called to a higher purpose; and be assured, we will often be called to stand alone against the rising tide of evil. When we do, we shouldn't expect the world to applaud. *"If the world hates you, you know that it hated Me* [Jesus] *before it hated you"* (John 15:18). Our hope is not in men but in the living God, who is the Savior of all men (see 1 Tim. 4:10).

PRAYER TO IGNITE

Thank You, God, that I have been set apart for a divine purpose. I choose to stand with You and fight the good fight.

TECHNIQUE

Rhythm is everything in boxing. Every move you make starts with your heart, and that's in rhythm or you're in trouble. —SUGAR RAY ROBINSON

If you want to learn technique...learn from a light guy. Learn from a guy who had to struggle and really learn how to do it correctly. —JOE ROGAN

...I fight like a boxer in the ring, not like someone who is shadowboxing (1 Corinthians 9:26 CEB).

Fight the good fight of faith, lay hold on eternal life, to which you were also called and have confessed the good confession in the presence of many witnesses (1 Timothy 6:12).

"BUT"

*...Indeed, now I know that there is no God in all
the earth, except in Israel...* (2 Kings 5:15).

*You face your greatest opposition when you're
closest to your biggest miracle.* —T.D. JAKES

Often, the most powerful, life-changing miracles seem to happen in the "buts" of life.

Consider the story of Naaman. Second Kings 5:1 describes him with glowing accolades:

Commander of the army of the king of Syria.

A great man with his master.

High favor.

A mighty man of valor.

Then out of nowhere, life-altering words: *But...he was a leper.*

Think about that. Leprosy. The most dreaded disease of his day—putrefying infected sores that in time caused loss of fingers, toes, nose. Leprosy was not a hidden disease. Everyone who came in contact with Naaman saw the miserable condition he carried with him. There was no hiding it. It was the first thing they saw. It defined him.

Many men are followers of Christ who love God, but they are defined by the "buts" in their lives. Maybe that's you. You love God and you really do believe that God loves you. You read the Word, pray, give your tithes and offerings, attend worship services, desiring to obey and walk in His Spirit.

But...

You aren't good enough.

But...

She said, "I don't love you anymore."

But...

We don't have a job for you.

But...

Your kid's an addict.

"Buts" that now seem to define who you are. "Buts" that perhaps even cause you to question God and His plan, even His goodness. "Buts" that understandably cause you to ask, "Where are You, God?"

Let's look again at the well-known Bible story of Naaman. At the recommendation of a young slave girl, he traveled to find the prophet Elisha. Elisha sends a servant out to instruct Naaman to go and wash seven times in the Jordan. Albeit reluctantly, and even with quite a bit of raging about how irrational the command is, he obeys.

I wonder how Naaman felt after he dunked himself the first time. No change. The second time. No change. Third time. No change. After number six, he might have been thinking that this was a horrible joke and a waste of time. The anger he had initially felt was returning. Someone was going to pay for this public act of embarrassment.

Have you been there? Faith…trust…obedience…and seemingly no change. You find yourself confused, distraught, and perhaps even a bit angry at God.

Then Naaman dipped the seventh time and "his flesh was restored like the flesh of a little child, and he was clean" (2 Kings 5:14 ESV). He went back to the "man of God," stood before him, and declared, *"Indeed, now I know that there is no God in all the earth, except in Israel; now therefore, please take a gift from your servant"* (2 Kings 5:15).

Though it seemed otherwise, God was in the midst of Naaman's pain, faithfully working His plan in the "but" of his life, which ultimately brought glory to Him. And God is in the midst of your pain also. He hasn't forgotten you. He hasn't forsaken you. He is faithfully working in the plan of your life. He's taking *your story* and making it *His story* for *His glory.*

Don't be defined by the "but" in your pilgrimage. Don't give up. Keep believing that He is God, and He is good. Your miracle could be just one more "dip in the Jordan" away—so keep dipping, my friend.

PRAYER TO IGNITE

Lord, grant me the strength to keep dipping for as long as it takes so You can be glorified in my life. Let my story be used for Your glory.

Day 32

JUST ABIDE

I am the vine, you are the branches. He who abides in Me, and I in him, bears much fruit; for without Me you can do nothing (John 15:5).

Train hard, but then let the performance flow naturally. Don't try to make something happen, just trust your stuff and let it happen. —GARY MACK, *Mind Gym*[1]

Do you believe that God's heart is for you?

That He's really there for you?

Really?

That He's got your back?

Men can do a host of religious activities, but they have a hard time inviting God into the deepest parts of themselves and practicing His presence. It is important for men to recognize God's calling on their lives and to have great expectations of what He will do. However, it's equally important to recognize that none of us can do anything worth doing without Him. When we attempt to accomplish God's work, or even live the Christian life, apart from an authentic relationship with Him, we get burned out, frustrated, and fail. It amounts to religion without relationship; but God created us for relationship. Dr. Henry Cloud notes:

> Relationship or bonding...is at the foundation of God's nature. Since we are created in His likeness, relationship is our most fundamental need, the very foundation of who we are. Without relationship, without attachment to God and others, we can't be ourselves.[2]

Any good work that is of lasting, eternal worth flows naturally out of a relationship with God. Our tendency as men is to grit our teeth and exert our willpower. We wrestle with ourselves toiling to do right, when our focus should not be on doing but on being—not struggling, but abiding. The problem with willpower, it doesn't work. Fruit is never the product of willpower. It's a result of abiding in the Vine. Galatians 5:22 says, *"But the fruit of the Spirit is love, joy, peace, longsuffering, kindness, goodness, faithfulness...."* Isn't that what we all want? It comes as a result of being with Jesus.

In the parable of the Sower, Jesus said whoever received seed on the good ground is the one who hears the Word and understands it and bears fruit (see Matt. 13:23). Let your efforts be directed to hearing the Word of God and then allowing the Holy Spirit guide you to understand it. Then, in relationship with Him, as you abide, the seeds of His Word will grow and produce fruit—lasting, eternal fruit.

Don't try harder to make it happen. Rest in what He's already done. Allow the Holy Spirit to flow through you and let it happen.

PRAYER TO IGNITE

God, I thank You that I am good ground and that every good work comes from abiding in You. Help me to hear Your words and understand them.

ENDNOTES

1. Gary Mack, *Mind Gym, An Athlete's Guide to Inner Excellence*, 183.
2. Henry Cloud, *Changes That Heal* (Grand Rapids, MI: Zondervan, 1992), Chapter 3.

VAPORS

*So teach us to number our days that we may
gain a heart of wisdom* (Psalm 90:12).

How did it get so late so soon? —Dr. Seuss

The modern day definition of the word "tragedy": being successful in the things that don't matter, especially with the time we have left on earth.

Listen.

Life will trash your trophies.

So what matters?

Who you love and who loved you. That's what matters—the love between you, God, and those He places close in your life.

It's about time. What you are doing with it.

According to a recent study, the most read sections of the average newspaper are the local news (65 percent) and the sports (59 percent). Guess which is the least read section? You got it. The obituaries. One of the reasons for that statistic is reading obituaries reminds people of the reality that they *too* are going to die. They don't want to think about it. Instead of facing reality, many men simply suppress the negative thoughts about death and go about their lives as if it's never going to happen. Yet, pondering one's own death or the preciousness of time is not negative. It's both wise and biblical. King David wrote in Psalm 90:12, *"So teach us to number our days, that we may gain a heart of wisdom."* Wisdom comes as we consider our mortality, ponder the time we have remaining, and ask God to show us how to make our days count.

James 4:14 says, *"Whereas you do not know what will happen tomorrow. For what is your life? It is even a vapor that appears for a little time and then vanishes away."* Even though you may not want to think about it, from an eternal perspective, a man's life is like a vanishing vapor. Here for a moment, then "puff" it's gone. But God has a purpose for our slight vapor of time. He has a plan and a time frame for its execution.

The enemy knows this. That's why he tries to keep us distracted and out of the fight. If he can keep us busy doing urgent things rather than important things, things that waste time, rather than maximizing our days, he's got us. Before we know it, "puff" we'll be gone and God's purpose for us unfulfilled. Ecclesiastes 9:12 gives us a firm warning:

> *For man also does not know his time: Like fish taken in a cruel net, like birds caught in a snare, so the sons of men are snared in an evil time, when it falls suddenly upon them.*

What have you been giving your heart to lately? Time is fleeting. Be alert and ready. Keep your guard up and your feet planted. Don't be caught in the enemy's snare. Ephesians 5:15-17 (NIV) says:

> Be very careful, then, how you live—not as unwise but as wise, making the most of every opportunity, because the days are evil. Therefore do not be foolish, but understand what the Lord's will is.

PRAYER TO IGNITE

> Lord, teach me to number my days like David. Help me to understand Your will for me and to be wise with the time I have, making the most of the important opportunities that You are bringing before me.

VERBAL PUNCHES

*Even so the tongue is a little member
and boasts great things. See how great a
forest a little fire kindles! (James 3:5)*

*Cold words freeze people, and hot words scorch
them, and bitter words make them bitter, and
wrathful words make them wrathful. Kind words
also produce their image on men's souls; and a
beautiful image it is. They smooth, and quiet,
and comfort the hearer.* —BLAISE PASCAL

Wildfires burning out of control.

We've all seen the devastation on the news.

Acres and acres of beautiful forests, multimillion-dollar homes, and more importantly, lives, all destroyed by the raging fires. What's interesting is that in almost all of the cases, these massive wildfires started from just a single spark. Someone dropped a cigarette butt or left some coals on a campfire and the wind kicked it up. Four out of five wildfires are started by humans. It's hard to imagine that such devastation begins with a seemingly insignificant little spark. But the damage produced by that spark will be visible for several decades.

While out-of-control fires can be devastating, in the right place they can be warm and inviting. So it is with our tongue. Ever since kindergarten we have been taught the old adage, "Sticks and stones may break my bones, but words can never hurt me." Don't believe it. It's not true. Words have power—power to encourage, create, transform, or hurt, tear, and destroy. Our tongue is a fire. Proverbs 18:21 says, *"Death and life are in the power of the tongue."*

You can speak death into someone or you can speak life into someone. *New York Times* bestselling author Helen Yglesias's brother's words broke her spirit. When Helen was a teenager during the Great Depression, she aspired to be a writer. She started writing a book and was excited about it. She eagerly let her brother read her manuscript, expecting encouragement and even a bit of constructive criticism. But his response almost destroyed Helen. "Nobody in the world is going to be interested in that &$#@* stuff you're writing," he said brashly. "You'd have to be a genius to get away with this boring stuff, and you're no genius."

Frustrated and hurt, Helen ripped her manuscript to shreds. Those words, spoken by her insensitive brother, caused a forty-year delay in Helen Yglesias's writing career. But after that long delay, Helen couldn't take it anymore and, with the constant encouragement of a friend, finally wrote her book. The book became a *New York Times* bestseller and she went on to write many other bestsellers!

We all go through life with a remarkable power right under our nose. It is a power so great that it is capable of producing life or death depending on how it's used. What about you? What are your words producing?

> *Out of the same mouth proceed blessing and cursing. My brethren, these things ought not to be so* (James 3:10).

> *Pleasant words are as an honeycomb, sweet to the soul, and health to the bones* (Proverbs 16:24 KJV).

PRAYER TO IGNITE

Lord Jesus, thank You for the people in my life. Please forgive me for the many times when I have spoken words that did not bring life. Please help me to build people up with my words today.

Day 35

PRESS ON

*I press on toward the goal for the prize of the upward
call of God in Christ Jesus* (Philippians 3:14 ESV).

*I'm a firm believer in goal setting. Step by step.
I can't see any other way of accomplishing
anything.* —MICHAEL JORDAN

At the start of the 1980 Winter Olympics in Lake Placid,
New York, the U.S. hockey team was little more than
an afterthought.

The Soviets were seeded number 1, and deservedly so.
They had won five gold medals and one bronze in the previous six Olympics.

The U.S. team was seeded seventh.

The Soviets unleashed 30 shots in the first two periods
to the United States 10. One dramatic save after another by
goaltender Jim Craig kept the U.S. team close.

Mark Johnson scored with one second remaining in
the first period to tie it at 2 all, but the Soviets led 3-2 after
two periods.

Team member John Harrington was quoted later as saying, "We'd played 40 minutes, they were just one ahead, but we were younger. *We wanted to take it to 'em!*"

Johnson tied it again 8:39 into the third period. At the 10 minute mark, Mike Eruzione, team captain, took Harrington's pass from the corner and unleashed a shot past a Russian defenseman and through the goalie into the net.

The explosion of cheers was deafening, and most of the 10,000 fans began to chant, "USA! USA!" that did not end for the final 10 minutes.

At the final buzzer, against seemingly insurmountable odds, the U.S. team was victorious.

After the game, coach Herb Brooks pulled a yellow card from his pocket with the scrawled message on it that he had read to his team just before the game: "*You were born to be a player. You were meant to be here.*"

What's interesting is that the U.S. team was not playing to win the gold medal. That game was two days later (which they won). They were simply putting it all on the line against the best team they had ever played.

If you have ever seen the movie *Miracle,* you will remember the portrayal of young men with unyielding determination to excel—to be excellent, to be the best they could be.

Our faith-walk is no different. The apostle Paul says, that like an Olympian runner, we are to strive in life to "*press* [earnestly endeavor to acquire] *on toward the goal for the prize of the upward call of God in Christ Jesus"* (Phil. 3:14 ESV).

Consider these other verses of challenge in your journey to excellence:

> *Whatever your hand finds to do, do it with all your might...* (Ecclesiastes 9:10 NASB).

> *But as you excel in everything—in faith, in speech, in knowledge, in all earnestness, and in our love for you...* (2 Corinthians 8:7 ESV).

> *And he [Jesus] said to him, "You shall love the Lord your God with all your heart and will all your soul and with all your mind"* (Matthew 22:37 ESV).

In First Corinthians, Paul admonishes the church in Corinth to be *"always abounding in the work of the Lord"* (1 Cor. 15:58 ESV). The word translated "abounding" *(perisseuo)* literally means outstanding, doing over and above, excelling.

No matter what, do your best. Be your best. Strive for excellence. Excel! And always keep your heart and mind centered on Him.

> *"...work hard and with gladness all the time, as though working for Christ, doing the will of God with all your hearts"* (Ephesians 6:7 TLB).

PRAYER TO IGNITE

Lord, I work for You. Though I know I can never repay You for what You've done for me. Everything I am or will be is because of Your grace in my life. Help me to do my work for Your glory and honor You with my effort. It's my reasonable service.

Day 36

GOD NEVER WASTES A WOUND

He said to me, "My grace is sufficient for you, for My strength is made perfect in weakness..." (2 Corinthians 12:9).

God uses...weakness, along with other afflictions, as his chisel for sculpting our lives. Felt weakness deepens dependence on Christ for strength each day. The weaker we feel, the harder we lean. And the harder we lean, the stronger we grow spiritually... To live with your "thorn" uncomplainingly—that is, sweet, patient, and free in heart to love and help others, even though every day you feel weak—is true sanctification. It is true healing for the spirit. It is a supreme victory of grace. —J.I. PACKER[1]

Growing up without a dad.

The death of a child.

A broken marriage.

Not making the team...

Even self-inflicted wounds…

An affair.

Too busy.

Lost in work.

Addictions.

And more…

Some wounds go deeper than others. Some have scabbed over. The enemy loves to pick at our scabs. When he does, the pain blinds us and we get lost. We can get so overwhelmed that we lose sight of the fact that God often uses our pain as part of our personal journey. Going through times of suffering allows us to have mercy on and help others who are in pain. It also helps us to depend on God. *"…But this happened,"* said the apostle Paul, *"that that we might not rely on ourselves but on God, who raises the dead"* (2 Cor. 1:9 NIV). What happened? Here's what happened, *"…We were under great pressure, far beyond our ability to endure, so that we despaired of life itself"* (2 Cor. 1:8 NIV). You'd think it was the good times that taught Paul to depend on God who raises the dead, but that's not what he said. It was the rough times, the times when he was pressured beyond his ability that taught him to depend on God. So it is with us.

Paul was no stranger to suffering. He was buffeted by the evil one and prayed for God to rid him of his thorn in the flesh. It was a burden to him. *"Concerning this thing I pleaded with the Lord three times that it might depart from me"* (2 Cor. 12:8). If you're in a place where, like Paul, you've pleaded for God to remove *that thing* in your life (you know what it is) but He hasn't, take comfort. Paul learned that in his weakness God's strength is made strong in him (see 2 Cor. 12:9).

God never wastes a wound. He uses them to teach us wisdom and show us how to avoid going through those things again. He uses them to draw us back to Him, *for when we are weak then He is strong* (see 1 Cor. 4:10). We also take the comfort we received from God and in-turn become conduits of comfort to others. Second Corinthians 1:3-4 says:

> *Blessed be the God and Father of our Lord Jesus Christ, the Father of mercies and God of all comfort, who comforts us in all our tribulation, that we may be able to comfort those who are in any trouble, with the comfort with which we ourselves are comforted by God.*

The great need in the world today is not for more gifted men or more talented men, but for more broken men. Why? Because God delights in taking cracked vessels, comforting them, and then using those vessels to bring comfort to a dying world. We become conduits through which His healing virtue flows.

PRAYER TO IGNITE

God, You are my strength. When I am weak, You make me strong. I thank You that when trials come my way I can take comfort in You. Help me not to waste my wounds, but to take the comfort that You have given me and become a conduit of comfort to others.

ENDNOTE

1.   http://www.goodreads.com/quotes/215182-god-uses-chronic
      -pain-and-weakness-along-with-other-afflictions; accessed
      6/5/14.

GOD, WHAT'S GOING ON HERE?

Wait for the Lord; be strong, and let your heart take courage; wait for the Lord! (Psalm 27:14 ESV)

The problem with waiting is that when we wait, we think that nothing is happening. The truth is that if we are waiting on God, all kinds of things are happening. —STEVE FARRAR[1]

God, what's going on here?

Nothing makes any sense.

We've been waiting for You to show up.

I didn't even do anything wrong, and look at the mess I'm in.

Have you ever felt that way? Asked those questions? I know I have. Understand that your current circumstance could be because of what you've done *right!* You desire to know God on a deeper level. You've prayed for Him to increase your effectiveness. Maybe He's answering your request. Read what Psalm 105 says about Joseph's life:

He [God] called down famine on the land and destroyed all their supplies of food; and he sent a man before them—Joseph, sold as a slave. They bruised his feet with shackles, his neck was put in irons, till what he foretold came to pass, till the word of the Lord proved him true" (Psalm 105:16-19 NIV).

There are seasons in our lives when God allows famine to touch us. It could be physical or spiritual—a season when we seem to be starving for more of God. God used the famine in Egypt to further His purposes. He stirs up a hunger to know Him more by allowing us to experience spiritual famines for a season.

God had given Joseph a dream that he was destined for greatness, that he would be a ruler, even over his brothers. In youthful excitement he shared this with his brothers. They were less than thrilled and you know what happened. They sold Joseph as a slave and told his father that he'd been killed (see Gen. 37).

But in his heart, Joseph held on to the dream God had given him, and his faith was tried, *"till what he foretold came to pass, till the word of the Lord proved him true."* Joseph's faith was tried with ten to fifteen years of waiting and delays, of mistreatment and imprisonment even though he was innocent. During those years in prison I'm sure Joseph entertained thoughts like, "I wonder if I missed God. Maybe those dreams were just my own imagination. I must have been delusional to think that God was really speaking to me."

I wrote this in my *Break Through* book:

> When we feel alone, wondering where God could possibly be, we can know that he's as close as our breath, he loves us dearly, and he has our best interests at heart. Often, he doesn't rescue us out of our predicaments. Instead, his purpose is very different. He's not committed to our comfort, but to deepening our trust in him. His training always includes times of light and times of darkness.[2]

The whole time Joseph was in prison, God was working. He was working out the details and He was working on Joseph. By the time of Joseph's release from prison, he was a completely different man. No longer was he the impulsive guy who needed to divulge all he was envisioning and perceiving. God had used this time of waiting to cultivate in Joseph a quiet confidence that prepared him to rule over Egypt and his brothers with humility and grace. This is what God desires to cultivate in us also.

> *The fruit of that righteousness will be peace; its effect will be quietness and confidence forever* (Isaiah 32:17).

The fruit of righteousness comes from abiding in the Vine—Jesus Christ (see John 15). Soaking in His Word. Dwelling in His presence. Walking in the Spirit. Obeying the promptings of the Holy Spirit. Staying mindful that He is working *all things for good for those who love God and are called according to His purpose* (see Rom. 8:28). Settling in with a resolve that your faith and hope are in Christ as He builds His character deep down inside you. Sinking deeper in love with Him as you see Him come through for you time and time again. Resting in the knowledge that His Word is truth, that although we can't see Him, He can see us. He knows the way we take (see Job 23:8-10). Trusting Him to bring about His will and purpose in our lives as we abide in Him.

God sees you.

He is with you. He is in the midst of it all.

You *will* get through this.

PRAYER TO IGNITE

God, Your ways are higher than my ways and Your thoughts above mine. I believe You are using all things in my life, even delays, to bring about Your will in my life. Train me as I go through those times of light and darkness.

ENDNOTES

1. Steve Farrar, *Gettin' There—How a Man Finds His Way on the Trail of Life* (Sisters, OR: Multnomah Books, 2001), 90.
2. Tim Clinton, *Break Through—When to Give In, How to Push Back* (Brentwood, TN: Worthy Publishing, 2012), 273.

ENCOUNTERS OF THE GOD KIND

*When they saw the courage of Peter and John
and realized that they were unschooled, ordinary
men, they were astonished and they took note that
these men had been with Jesus* (Acts 4:13 NIV).

*I was so overwhelmed at seeing and feeling
Jesus' presence so close. At one point I turned
around and looked over my shoulder as if He was
standing there.* —Astronaut James Irwin

Apollo 15 Astronaut James Irwin had an encounter of the God kind...on the Moon. That's right, on the Moon. Standing on the surface of the "blue planet," as he called it, gazing at the spectacular beauty of the Earth some 238,000 miles away, Irwin experienced the nearness of Jesus Christ in a profound way, unlike anything he'd ever felt before on Earth. Jesus' presence was so tangible, Irwin said, *"at one point I turned around and looked over my shoulder as if He was standing there."* Then, right there on the moon, Jesus spoke to Irwin and gave him a new assignment.

Now you may be reading this and thinking, "Who wouldn't have an emotional experience in that incredible setting? The euphoria had to have been out of this world!" However, this was much more than an emotional experience. This encounter with the living Christ changed James Irwin's life forever. God encounters tend to do that. Before his mission to the Moon, Irwin considered himself a "nominal" Christian at best. He was disengaged from the fight.

As a result of his lunar encounter with God, however, Irwin experienced a new courage and boldness to witness for Jesus Christ. He was also given a new assignment and got back in the fight! Within a year of his return from space, Irwin resigned from NASA and formed High Flight Foundation, a missionary organization with the purpose of reaching the world as "goodwill ambassadors of the Prince of Peace."[1]

As a man fully engaged in this fight, you are going to need encounters with the living God that impart courage and power for you to carry out your assignment. Here's the good news; you don't have to be on the Moon for Jesus to show up. He'll meet you wherever you are, in any circumstance. Once, Jesus met Peter in the middle of the night during a raging storm. The disciple's boat was being pounded and in jeopardy of sinking. When they saw Jesus coming toward them walking on the water, they thought He was a ghost and cried out in fear.

> *But Jesus immediately said to them: "Take courage! It is I. Don't be afraid." "Lord, if it's you," Peter replied, "tell me to come to you on the water."*

"Come," he said. Then Peter got down out of the boat, walked on the water and came toward Jesus (Matthew 14:27-29 NIV).

In the midst of the brutal gale, Jesus told Peter and the rest of the disciples, *"Take courage! It is I."* Just like with James Irwin, one of the things imparted to us when we have encounters with the living God, is courage. Then, He gives us a new assignment. Jesus told Peter to *"Come."* As a result, Peter stepped out of his boat of security and as long as his eyes were fixed on Jesus, he walked on the water. If you are going to walk on water, you've got to get out of the boat. The question is, what's holding you back?

Jesus is still showing up today, often in the midst of our most difficult storms. Sometimes it's even on the Moon! As we encounter Him in a personal way, Jesus is calling us to take courage, to step out of our boats of security and trust Him. When we do, we will experience supernatural power to do those things He's calling us to do. As we are walking on the water with our eyes firmly focused on Jesus, we'll know the power is from Him and not ourselves. Most importantly, people will take note that we are ordinary men who've had an encounter with the living Jesus.

When they saw the courage of Peter and John and realized that they were unschooled, ordinary men, they were astonished and they took note that these men had been with Jesus (Acts 4:13 NIV).

PRAYER TO IGNITE

God, I cling to Your hand. I need a living encounter with You to sustain me in this fight. Keep me and don't let me go. You are my Source for everything. I want to walk with You.

ENDNOTE

1.   http://www.godreports.com/testimony-view/1249; accessed 6/5/14.

WHAT KEEPS YOU AWAKE AT NIGHT?

Therefore do not worry about tomorrow, for tomorrow will worry about its own things. Sufficient for the day is its own trouble (Matthew 6:34).

Fear in the mind leads to anxiety in the body, reducing the quality and duration of life. Our God is able to sympathize with us because he's been here. He is a good Dad who knows we have needs. He'll take care of us. —MARK DRISCOLL

About 90 million Americans have trouble with sleep. Many of them try, or get hooked on, all kinds of remedies— Tylenol PM, Benadryl, NyQuil, Ambien. I'm certainly not anti-medication; sleep aides sometimes are necessary and ok. But why take them if you don't need them? How about we look at what are the reasons for your sleeping difficulties? At the core, most sleep problems are associated with a mind that won't quit—a heavy heart, to do lists, problems or challenges.

If it's physical, maybe you need to try some exercise or cutting back on your caffeine during the day. Read a book before turning out the light. Maybe seeing a doctor or professional counselor is in order. But if your source of insomnia is worry and anxiousness, you need to take it to the Almighty Counselor. Jehovah Shalom—our God of Peace who transcends all understanding, who is *"able to do exceedingly abundantly above all that we ask or think, according to the power that works in us"* (Eph. 3:20).

Philippians 4:6-7 tells us to:

> *Be anxious for nothing, but in everything by prayer and supplication, with thanksgiving, let your requests be made known to God; and the peace of God, which surpasses all understanding, will guard your hearts and minds through Christ Jesus.*

Here we are told to be anxious for nothing and to give everything over to God—all those things you've been carrying in your mind. Don't worry over stuff that may happen or has already happened. Losing sleep over these things can make you crazy. We serve the God who can be trusted to keep that which we have committed to Him (see 2 Tim. 1:12). When you lay down at night turn everything you've been carrying over to Him. Get back to counting sheep and let it go. God's got your back! He's the Shepherd.

Think in the morning. Act in the noon. Eat in the evening. Sleep in the night. —William Blake

PRAYER TO IGNITE

Holy Spirit, fill me with Your peace that passes all understanding. Help me to turn my cares over to You and trust in You. Help me to wake rested and refreshed so I can be most effective for You.

Day 40

LET'S ROLL!

I have fought a good fight, I have finished my course, I have kept the faith (2 Timothy 4:7 KJV).

We all knew what kind of person Todd was. ...Just knowing that when the crisis came up he maintained the same character we all knew, it's a testament to what real faith means. —LISA BEAMER[1]

Todd Beamer...remember him? We should. None of us should ever forget. A true hero of September 11, 2001, he led the guys who stormed the cockpit of United Flight 93 and took down three terrorist hijackers. Their courageous choice to fight back foiled the plot to missile the Boeing 757 into the White House. Instead, the plane crashed into an open field outside Shanksville, Pennsylvania. The heroic act surely saved hundreds, if not thousands of lives. It came at a price though, the sacrifice of their own. After becoming aware that three other planes had flown into the Twin Towers in New York and the Pentagon building in Washington, the 38 passengers and crew, made the choice.

Before taking action, Todd had conversed with GTE in-flight telephone operator Lisa Jefferson. She could hear shouts and commotion in the background as Todd explained their plans to overtake the hijackers. The pilot and co-pilot had been wounded or killed and were unable to fly the plane. While panic and confusion filled the background, Jefferson noted that extreme peace emanated from Todd.

When the time arrived, Todd, Jeffery Glick, Thomas Brunett Jr., and Mark Bingham, all in their thirties, knew for certain what had to be done. Todd prayed a short prayer with Jefferson, asked her to tell his family that he loved them, and left the line open. Not long afterward, Jefferson heard Todd's voice saying, "Let's roll!" Then there was silence.

It took courage, confidence, and faith for Todd Beamer to take action and lead in that moment. The phrase "Let's roll" was not a spur of the moment thing. No. According to his wife Lisa, he always said that. It was Todd's mantra, part of his lifestyle. And it rubbed off on those around him. "My boys even say that," Lisa said. "When we're getting ready to go somewhere, we say, 'C'mon guys, let's roll.' My little one says, 'C'mon, Mom, let's roll.' That's something they picked up from Todd."

Todd Beamer lived his faith in the little things. He was engaged in the daily fight. Then, when it was his time to take action in a big way, to throw a knockout punch, it was only a natural extension of who he was as a man. Todd could respond courageously, because courage was in his core and that's what this devotional has been all about—having the courage to get back in the fight and stand firm in the face of the enemy until the very end.

Our goal in life should be to finish strong, not disengage or quit. The enemy's goal is to get us to quit the fight. If we give up, he's got us. You may be bone weary, but don't give up. Reach down deep. You've still got some punches left. Let God refresh you, empower you, train your *hands for war, and fingers for battle!* Like Todd Beamer, *"Remember the Lord, who is great and awesome, and fight for your brethren, your sons, your daughters, your wives, and your homes"* (Neh. 4:14 ESV), even if that means laying down your life.

Regardless where you are in your personal journey, God can redeem the time. Joel 2:25 (KJV) states that God *"will restore to you the years that the locust hath eaten...."* Throw yourself back in the ring! Trust Him again and you too can say along with the apostle Paul, *"I have fought a good fight, I have finished my course, I have kept the faith."*

Hopefully, on this 40-day journey you have picked up some valuable tools to assist you in your own fight. God is saying it is time to *ignite* a passion back in you, to get your fire back. The truth is, you're at a fork in the road.

What are you going to do?

Make your choice and "Let's roll!"

PRAYER TO IGNITE

Father, I want to fight the good fight of faith and finish strong. I want to be a man after Your own heart. Train my hands for war and my fingers for battle as I struggle to serve You. Help me to stand and fight for my wife, my family, and for the purpose that You've called me to. Let me not lose sight of who I am in Christ—a champion.

ENDNOTE

1. http://old.post-gazette.com/headlines/20010916phonecallnat3p3.asp; accessed 6/5/14.

...Do not be afraid of them. Remember the Lord, who is great and awesome, and fight for your brothers, your sons, your daughters, your wives, and your homes (Nehemiah 4:14 ESV).

ACKNOWLEDGMENTS

Max Davis, a contender...someone who understands what it means to fight every day for what matters. I've so enjoyed our time together on this book and our developing friendship and camaraderie.

Team 'Destiny Image', Joel Nori and Curtis Wallace—thanks for believing in this project. It's a joy to work with you, and I sincerely appreciate your vision for discipling and ministering to men.

My family...Julie, Megan and Ben, and Zach, you are a daily inspiration and encouragement to me. I love my life with you all.

ABOUT THE AUTHORS

 **TIM CLINTON**, Ed. D., is President of the nearly 50,000-member American Association of Christian Counselors (AACC), the largest and most diverse Christian counseling association in the world. He is Professor of Counseling and Pastoral Care, and Executive Director of the Center for Counseling and Family Studies at Liberty University. Licensed in Virginia as both a Professional Counselor (LPC) and Marriage and Family Therapist (LMFT), Tim now spends a majority of his time working with Christian leaders and professional athletes. He is recognized as a world leader in faith and mental health issues and has authored over 20 books including *Breakthrough: When to Give In, When to Push Back*. Most importantly, Tim has been married 33 years to his wife Julie and together they have two children, Megan (recently married to Ben Allison) and Zach. For more information, visit www.TimClinton.com and www.AACC.net.

 **MAX DAVIS** holds degrees in Journalism and Biblical Studies. He is the author of over twenty books of both fiction and non-fiction. His books have been translated into several languages and have been featured on shows such as *The 700 Club*, *The Today Show*, and in *USA Today*. He and his wife Alanna live on thirty beautiful acres in Greenwell Springs, LA. To learn more, visit www.MaxDavisBooks.com.

INCLUDED IN MEMBERSHIP

Christian Counseling Today
Our flagship quarterly publication tackles the most pressing issues facing counselors and pastors. With its uniquely Christian point of view, *Christian Counseling Today* delves into today's hottest and most controversial subjects, offering analysis that is thought-provoking, clinically-excellent and biblically-sound.

Christian Counseling Connection
Our top-quality and recognized quality newsletter features professional reports and gives you the latest news, research and developments in the biblical counseling field. This succinct newsletter also features membership activities, promotes forthcoming conferences and addresses clinical, pastoral, lay, international and student issues.

Counsel CDs
This quarterly interview feature focuses on relevant topics in biblical counseling by experts in our field and is ready for your CD player when you have time for learning.

Presidential Insights
Join in on scheduled calls (quarterly), when AACC President, Dr. Tim Clinton, will discuss relevant topics and how they impact the current state of Christian counseling, as well as answer your questions.

AACC eNews
This monthly, Web-based electronic journal is geared to your needs and practice as a 21st century counselor providing up-to-the-minute news and views on important events and developments.

Member Discounts
Members receive registration discounts on popular conferences, as well as discounts on Continuing Education Credits, counseling resources, and books.

Counseling Resource Catalog
Recognized by the American Psychological Association, National Board for Certified Counselors, and most states. Through our conferences, publications and training programs, there are numerous opportunities available.

Opportunities for Continuing Education
Earn CE Credits through our conferences, webinars, publications and training programs with preferred pricing for members.

You will also receive a **Member Benefits Card** and **Certificate of Membership** suitable for framing.